A Juicy
JOYFUL
Life

Inspiration from Women
Who've Found the *sweetness* in Every Day

Here's to your
juicy joyful life!
Love + Light,
Ellie B

Published by Inspired Living Publishing, LLC.
P.O. Box 1149, Lakeville, MA 02347

ISBN-13: 978-0-9845006-0-4
ISBN-10: 0-9845006-0-x

Library of Congress Control Number: 2010911210

www.InspiredLivingPublishing.com
(508) 265-7929

Cover and Layout Design: Rachel Dunham, www.HummingbirdCreativeConcepts.com

Editor: Bryna René, Aphrodite, Inc. www.wordsbyaphrodite.com

Printed in the United States.

Dedication

This book is dedicated to…

Every woman: may you discover the divine truth within, and step forward to shine your light brightly, illuminating the path of self-discovery for others to follow.

My daughter Niki: thanks for being the beautiful, amazing woman you are. Your love continues to illuminate my path and transform my life. Shine Brightly!

Rachel Dunham, graphic designer extraordinaire, who has an innate gift for bringing my visions to life.

Project Manager and web guru Kim Turcotte of Grow Your Divine Business, who has a gift for breaking down the big picture into bite-sized pieces.

Editor Bryna René, who brought this book to life with ease and grace.

Shann Vander Leek, visionary and mastermind partner, whose shining example we can all benefit from following.

…And finally, to all the countless others who have assisted me with this project: my heartfelt gratitude for seeing the mission behind this endeavor, and stepping forward to support it.

PRAISE FOR A Juicy, Joyful Life

"*A Juicy, Joyful Life* is a stirring and soulful book to be savored, written in, dog-eared, and shared with friends. Read any story in this remarkable collection and you will be transported to a world that will make you laugh, cry, and grow beyond your self-imposed limits. You will know without a shadow of a doubt that you already are who you always were."

– **Kat Tansey**, award-winning author of *Choosing to Be: Lessons in Living from a Feline Zen Master*

"My personal experience leaves me with no doubt whatsoever that authentically sharing our struggles and our victories brings freedom, joy, and inspiration to storytellers and listeners alike. *A Juicy, Joyful Life* is chock full of uplifting stories, each one followed by a series of thoughtful questions that help readers translate their inspiration into something personal and actionable. Congratulations, Linda, on 'walking the talk' of authenticity, purpose, and passion to create a beautiful gift for women all over the world"

– **Andrea Howe**, creator of *Hear Us Roar! 28 Stories of Everyday Women Leading Extraordinary Lives*

"In our insane quest for perfection, we women tend to dab makeup on our scars so that no one will see. These brave souls rip off their scabs and show us that bleeding has an upside: it means we are alive. I wish I had been able to surround myself with women who were this honest when I was a girl! Buy this book so you can cry and tingle and laugh out loud; then, share both the book and yourself with a younger woman. For as long as we live, we can follow and share the examples of the women featured in *A Juicy, Joyful Life* and choose love, joy, and healing."

– **Sharon Roy**, woman, mother, author, farmer, life coach, and CEO

"*A Juicy, Joyful Life*'s powerful collection of life-changing moments is wonderful. A truly great book brings tears and laughter, followed by empowering new thoughts and inspired action. This book has it all and more!"

– **Yvonne Oswald**, best-selling, award-winning author of *Every Word has Power*

"A Juicy, Joyful Life is like wrapping yourself up in a big blanket of self-love that has you bursting from the inside out to be, love, and live the woman you truly are. The stories she delivers will spark your soul and fire up your heart... Yum!"
– **Christine Arylo**, author of *Choosing ME Before WE, Every Woman's Guide to Life and Love*

"A Juicy, Joyful Life is filled to the brim with loving reminders that when life hands you a lemon you can *choose* to make lemonade. Savor this book. Squeeze all the wisdom you can through the journaling prompts. Make powerful choices. Your juicy, joyful life is calling!"
– **Gina Bell**, Founder of IAWBO.com, The International Association of Women in Business Online

"A Juicy, Joyful Life takes you into the minds, hearts, and stories of women who have felt their inner pain, moved through their healing, and expanded into their joy. Find guidance and inspiration for your journey in this insightful book."
– **Lisa Michaels**, President, Natural Rhythms Institute

"The stories of these women—at some of the juiciest moments of their lives—spoke to me deeply. The journaling prompts make *A Juicy, Joyful Life* more than a book: it's a mentor, guide, and loving teacher to help readers access their inner wisdom in moments of challenge and change."
– **Lisa Tener**, national book coach, author

"This a book that can spur you on to make the most invincible choices in your life. I love the stories, the honesty, the comfort, and the brightness in these pages. I felt like I got to go to a conference, or a coaching session, or to dinner with a wise friend who had just chosen more for herself—and was going to make sure I did the same!"
– **Tama J. Kieves,** best-selling author of *This Time I Dance! Creating the Work You Love*

"A Juicy, Joyful Life touched my heart by allowing it to open more widely to be my authentic self. Linda, your passion for making a difference in the world is an inspiring example for all of us; your book has enriched my life more than you will ever know."
– **Joanie Winberg**, CEO, National Association of Divorce for Women and Children

"A Juicy, Joyful Life is a powerful testimony to love. Squeezed into every page are slices of inspiration honoring the many facets of life. Each zesty story presents beautifully crafted mirrors affirming that within every woman sleeps a goddess. This book is a gift; reminding you that life can be as sweet as you make it."
– **Elizabeth Harper**, author of *Wishing: How to Fulfill Your Heart's Desires*

"This book is the companion and community that every woman needs in her journey from spiritual awakening to living fully in her purpose. In these pages are insights and wisdom from women sharing the path to a more loving, joyful, and juicy life."
– **Alice Greene**, author of *Inspired to Feel Good: Making Healthy and Fit Choices So Rewarding and Liberating You Never Want to Stop*

"Much more than a collection of inspiring stories, Linda Joy's *A Juicy, Joyful Life* explores the lives of extraordinary women who had the strength and courage to see the light ahead when all else appeared dark. Each empowering story encourages the reader to break away from old patterns and embrace and release the powerful woman living inside. Supportive and encouraging, Linda invites the reader to see the parallels in each story shared and take a personal journey to apply the message into their life through useful tips and thought-provoking questions."
– **Kala Ambrose**, Explore Your Spirit radio host and author of *9 Life Altering Lessons: Secrets of the Mystery Schools Unveiled*

"The words on each page of *A Juicy, Joyful Life* were singing to me, familiar songs heard on my own personal journey, yet with new verses that tugged at my heartstrings. An immediate sisterhood was created with authors I have yet to meet but whose stories touched me deeply; kindred spirits brought together in this most inspiring and uplifting piece of work."
– **Leslie Sturgeon**, founder and President, Women Inspiring Women, New Hampshire's largest women's networking organization

"If you want to be happy, take these mind vitamins now! Linda Joy does it again! *A Juicy, Joyful Life* gives you every tool and resource to rise above your problems. Turn your sour into sweet, and embrace the life you'll love."
– **Deb Scott**, award-winning author of *The Sky is Green and The Grass is Blue— Turning Your Upside Down World Right Side Up!*

"Thank you, Linda Joy, for gathering these stories of pain and perseverance, triumph and transformation. This book offers a simple yet profound gift: the inspiration and healing power of women sharing their journeys."
– **Abby Seixas**, author of *Finding the Deep River Within: A Woman's Guide to Recovering Balance and Meaning in Everyday Life*

"Traditionally, grandmothers, mothers, and sisters have told their stories, passing their wisdom along the sacred web of life. When a woman shares her story, her pain can enrich us. When she doesn't share her story, her pain can kill her. A woman's story can light the spark of a thousand women. Linda Joy is that woman, and her book *A Juicy, Joyful Life* is that spark."
– **Shakaya Leone**, author of *Naked Beauty* and founder of EarthEmpress.com

"If you are ready to be daring, boldly make the choice of feeling juicy, and live the life of your wildest dreams, your journey starts right here. Open the first page of *A Juicy, Joyful Life* and savor the juicy inspiration of all the women who went before you. I recommend this book wholeheartedly to any woman who loves to wrap her arms around her joyful self and live passionately."
– **Saskia Roell**, transformational life coach and best-selling author of *A Suitcase Full of Faith: How One Woman Found Her Dream Following the Compass of her Soul*

"This is where the juice is! Ready to make your life delicious? Get this book! It is full of true heartfelt wisdom from real women and it lifts your worries away and leaves you with a yummy feeling inside. Give yourself a gift and get this book, you will be smiling in no time!"
– **Nan Akasha**, CHT, #1 best-selling author of *Already Rich! Secrets to Master Your Money Mind*

"If you are looking for inspiration and heart-filled stories that will change your life, this book is for you. I couldn't put the book down and was deeply touched by the honesty and depth of the stories written. Each story is filled with love and wisdom that will touch your heart and soul. I recommend it to all who are searching for a deeper spirituality and authentic juicy life."
– **Pat Hastings**, author of *Simply a Woman of Faith*

FOREWORD

BY REV. DR. Charlene Proctor

Spiritual growth, says Sri Bhagavan, always begins where you are, not where you want to be. This is his favorite advice, which he gives spiritual seekers who travel to India and want to shed their past traumas so they can move forward in life with strength and dignity. His goal is to show people who seek a relationship with the Divine the joy of a life that is free from pain. I've been there. I know it is entirely possible to empty our bodily containers of fear, regret, worry, self-doubt, and old emotional programming and conditioning and live in the present moment. But we must make a conscious decision to stop clinging to our old stories and reliving them. If we want to experience true freedom, we must be willing to give up our suffering and let go of fear. There is no room for personal or spiritual growth when our lives are polluted by the agonies of the past.

One of our greatest tasks is to be willing to experience uncertainty. Will we have enough? Will we be alone? What happens when we give up our old relationships? Old jobs? The uncertainty of making sudden and drastic change in our lives might look like we are choosing to run adrift, but that is only an outward appearance. It's an illusion, and not the truth of what is. There is no separation from our Source, which sustains us completely. Adopting a new attitude, achieving financial independence, choosing emotional self-reliance—these are only human rites of passage that help us release our worries so we can find the essence of what constitutes us as individuals. What is underneath is gorgeous and strong. How can this not be true when each of us is an individual spark of Divine creation?

Clearly, our individual and collective narratives are how Spirit experiences life through us. Contemplating our stories is where the learning resides, where the spiritual journey begins. Instead of regurgitating our fears and victimhood, what we ought to be doing is taking a closer look at the emerging wisdom arising from our everyday experiences.

In the East, we are taught that our external state always mirrors our internal state of consciousness. Our lives unfold according to the level of consciousness we choose. When we align with higher consciousness, we demonstrate positive values and easily manifest health and prosperity, our natural states. At that time, we can declare to the universe that we wish to link up with its loving presence, and then, all things are possible. We can manifest excellent health and healing, abundance and financial prosperity, and nurturing relationships.

Emotional healing, the kind that leads to the discovery of the vast quantity of space we have to fill with our authentic self, happens in many ways. For some of us, it is a mystical translation of energy, a downloading from the matrix of grace that washes us clean and gives us a blank page on which to write something new. For others, it is simply a willingness to *see*. In the oneness movement, we like to say, "To see is to be free," which means that we cannot truly discover our authentic self until we are willing to give up our suffering and pain, and toss away the dense lampshade that covers our natural light. When we are aware and *see*, we often discover that our mind, which is a tool we are supposed to use to navigate life, has enslaved us. It keeps looking for different solutions to the same old problems and keeps us in a state of unrest. A mind that is not at ease is one that favors the playing of old mental movies over and over again, always hoping for a different ending.

Freedom from the past begins when we decide to adopt a high level of thought-awareness. It takes discipline to achieve this state of awareness. Many spiritual students have agonized over the difficulties of quieting their over-active minds. But we cannot be at peace nor be at ease with ourselves without awareness. Breaking out of the depths of despair and moving into the juicy, joyful life that Linda Joy speaks about is the result of practicing awareness of the present. To live joyfully, we must give our attention to where we are at that moment and just *see*.

The power to lead a juicy life percolates in the present moment, not in yesterday or tomorrow, but *today*. Today is the first day of our journey toward authenticity. We can never experience freedom or bliss if we have no acceptance or appreciation of the present moment. The present moment is where the creative energy of the imagination resides, and we cannot be present with the joy of life that is ours if cannot experience people as they are without wrapping them up in layers of judgment or comparison. These old ideas about ourselves are made worse when we filter life through un-forgiveness. The hardest part comes from our inability to fill ourselves up with a sense of the Divine Presence, which is ultimately perfect in every way. A person who learns to work in conjunction with the Divine is authentic in every way. He or she is magnetic and expresses a level of confidence that inspires others. People who see the perfection of life are capable of seeing tragedy as a blessing. They can shift their perspective so that they can see the positive in any situation. It takes a lot of courage to override the mind's ongoing commentary and make a commitment to stop struggling.

When I read the stories in this book, I see women who have raised their consciousness. Their awareness of *what is* and their honesty with their struggles encourages us to re-examine our own human experiences. These women have experienced the full range of fear, and yet they rose above hate, insecurity, comparison, jealousy, anger, discontent, and pain. But rather than banish those emotions from their journeys, or worse, hang on to them as unwanted baggage, these women have given themselves permission to honor the gift each seemingly negative experience brings. In doing so, they have accepted Divine guidance and made themselves available to participating in a relationship with a higher power. They have chosen to be present. They have analyzed less and experienced more. They have invited grace into their lives.

Linda Joy and I have a common bond. Our passages from emotional poverty to empowerment have shown us that it is just as easy to see life as a collection of old wounds that contaminate our relationships as it is to see life as set of ideas that contribute to our emotional and spiritual growth. We both know that when old wounds fester, we develop attitudes and behaviors to cover them—a heavy armor that blocks us from fully experiencing life. This describes the despair of an unconscious existence, a self-chosen victimhood that translates into an inability to relate to people as they are. Linda and I have both liberated and empowered ourselves by sharing a vital message in our work: Come to terms with your past by letting go of it. Look for wisdom in where you are right now. To see order and disorder in all forms, practice awareness at the highest level. When you recognize disorder, take a deep breath and just move forward.

Life has an amazing quality that transforms us into extraordinary spiritual teachers who can encourage others to empower themselves with the wisdom of their everyday experiences. It's what this book is about. *A Juicy, Joyful Life* will show you that every woman can transform someone else when she shares her story. This book will encourage you to see reality as a wonderful opportunity to grow your passion for your work, your family, and yourself. And by sharing, you can rediscover your own reality.

Our ability to evolve arises from knowing our essence, our presence as consciousness, and consciousness is always *becoming aware of what is*. Spirit lives through us. It is an eternal presence that is never static. Our biggest challenge is to reinterpret life in such a way that we become wide-open channels for the Presence. This is when our natural state of being comes forth. The stories in this book will show you that you no longer have to see yourself as an object in the world; instead, you can see yourself as part of the eternal, infinite stuff which is God happening though you. When you see this truth, that is when you will begin to live the juicy and joyful life these women are writing about.

Remember that life is deliciously flavored with our uniqueness. We are safe and secure. We are loved beyond measure. All we have to do is move forward.

With every blessing,

Rev. Dr. Charlene M. Proctor
Bloomfield Hills, Michigan
August 2010

TABLE OF *Contents*

INTRODUCTION
by Linda Joy
PUBLISHER

T he sky, seen in patches through the budding branches of oak and maple trees, was the bluest of blues, the color of cornflowers. The scent of fresh-cut grass tickled my nostrils. I'd rolled all the windows down to let the spring air caress my face as I drove—but I didn't feel it. I didn't see the skies, or the trees, or notice the smell of new grass. All I could see through my tears was the dark blur of my steering wheel, and my fist as I pounded it on the dashboard, again and again.

I was going through one of the most painful, enraging, and transformational periods of my life. Long-buried childhood traumas were resurfacing, haunting me like restless ghosts: my innocence stolen, my bright spirit crushed before it ever had a chance to bloom. I felt like I was splitting open, ripped apart by the intensity of my emotions. I was terrified that I would never know who I was meant to be, because I was always going to be trapped in this vicious cycle of pain and anger, anger and pain. I was a single mom with a beautiful six-year-old daughter, and this pain was preventing me from being completely present for her. Not only was I failing myself; now, I was failing her. The torment was unbearable.

With sobs wracking my body, I pulled the car to the side of the road, and tried to compose myself. I had never been the kind of person who turned to a higher power. I never believed that there was a power available for me to turn to. But that day, I finally reached my breaking point. I shook my fist at Heaven, and let it all out, right there on the side of a tree-lined street. If there was a God, I decided, He was going to get an earful!

Twenty-nine years of anguish and shame came pouring out of me. I don't know how long I raged—an hour, maybe more—but when I came back to myself, still wiping my eyes with my tear-soaked tee shirt, I was completely spent. It was as if a huge reservoir of pain had been drained out of my heart, leaving an empty, gaping hole in its place.

What happened next still blows my mind.

Everything became very still. The breeze stopped. I could no longer hear the sound of lawn mowers in the distance, or the rustle of leaves overhead. I could feel my heart beating, and the way my breath hitched in my chest, but I was somehow beyond those things, as well. I basked in a deep, encompassing peace, a perfect stillness like I'd never experienced before.

And then, I heard it: the stern but also gentle and loving whisper which would transform my life, heal my heart, and allow me to begin to dance with my authentic self for the first time.

The voice said, "The experiences of your childhood do not erase the core of who you are. You have been here all along, but you have chosen not to see yourself. Instead, you've focused on the pain. You hold the power to become, at any time, whatever you desire to be. You can choose to live in the past, with all your pain and anger, or you can choose to be the bright, beautiful person at the core of who you are right now. So, what will you choose?"

Epiphany! Suddenly, my heart was filled with pure hope— a feeling I hadn't experienced in a long, long time. The wisdom I heard that day seemed so simple, so straightforward, but my heart resonated with the truth of it. I think the voice only reminded me of what I'd known, deep down, all along. I had a choice about my life, my feelings, my heartache.

So what did I want for myself? Who would I choose to be, if I was no longer a victimized child, a woman in pain?

A surge of energy coursed through me. I started ransacking my car, searching through the toys and napkins and bits of old French fries trapped in the seat crevices. Thoughts were coming fast and furious. Paper. I needed paper! In the end, all I had was a pen and a coffee-stained Dunkin' Donuts napkin, but they were enough. I started scribbling furiously.

This is what I wrote:

- I want to be loving
- I want to feel deserving
- I want to radiate love
- I want to be kind and trusting and filled with hope
- I want to experience true joy
- I want to know inner peace
- I want to experience self-love
- I want to make a difference in the world
- I want to forgive

This list, the expression of my heart's deepest desires, filled both sides of the napkin. Before that moment, I had never allowed myself to believe that any of those feelings were even possible for me, let alone accessible. But I had been made to see that anything was possible, and that I already held the key.

That spring day in 1991 was the day I took back my life. For years, that napkin stayed by my side wherever I went. Tattered, torn, and finally unreadable, it was my symbol of hope and transformation. That day, I set out on my journey to reclaim my authentic self—the self that had always been there, buried under my self-made mountain of pain and despair.

From that day forth, I spent every spare moment reading inspirational books from spiritual visionaries like Norman Vincent Peale, Florence Scovel Shinn, Napoleon Hill, and Ernest Holmes. They became my virtual mentors. As the years went by, I added to my transformational toolkit, soaking up the wisdom of teachers like Marianne Williamson, Tony Robbins, Debbie Ford, Cheryl Richardson, and dozens of others. I dedicated myself to living from the inside out, using the powers of my mind and heart to continually transform my life.

Nearly twenty years have passed, but my transformational journey continues to this day. I live a life of joy, ease, and love, because this is the life I choose for myself. My initial revelation, combined with the wisdom of the world's leading visionaries and "new thought" authors, has shaped my life's purpose, and brought me full circle. I am the founder and Publisher of *Aspire*, the leading women's inspirational magazine. Through *Aspire*—and now through Inspired Living Publishing—I am able to bring the transformational words and wisdom of visionaries, healers, spiritual warriors, and everyday women to readers around the globe.

Sixteen years ago, I met the man of my dreams, Dana, who has taught me more about authenticity and values than anyone else in my life. He continues to be my best friend and greatest teacher, and has been a wonderful role model for my amazing daughter, who is now twenty-six. I also have a stepson, Erik, and a truly exceptional ten-year-old grandson, Tyler.

Whenever I'm feeling stuck, or in need of a little boost, I have only to look back on how far I've come since that day when I sat in my car on the side of the road and shook my fist at God. My higher power had always been there, just waiting for me to look within.

4

What is A Juicy, Joyful Life?

A Juicy, Joyful Life is a life that celebrates the sweetness in every day. It's not a life you have to be born into, and it doesn't require a lot of money, or a nice house, or a fancy car. A Juicy, Joyful life is a life you choose for yourself—a life that celebrates your authenticity, savors every moment (whether sweet or sour), and which allows you space to grow and blossom.

A Juicy, Joyful Life is so much more than an anthology. Not only does this book bring to life the trials and triumphs of real women living authentic, inspiring lives; it invites you, the reader, to dive deeper into your own story. It is my hope that you will see yourself on these pages, and get a glimpse of the limitless possibilities available to you when you choose to live your truth from the inside out.

I believe that all women have an innate wisdom which transcends religion, age, race, and upbringing. Through the sharing of our stories, we have the power to uplift, inspire, and heal other women so that they, too, can overcome any obstacle. Through *Aspire*, this anthology (and its sisters to come), and my inspirational e-book series *Wisdom for Women*, I am thrilled to provide a venue for women to be heard and understood.

This project is the culmination of a dream for me. I have always envisioned a publishing company dedicated solely to women's inspiration, with a mission to bring women's stories to life—and with a little help and a lot of faith, we've created it. The book you hold in your hands is one more piece of proof that anything is possible, as long as you believe!

With love,

Linda Joy

BREAKING THROUGH—
The "Ah-ha!"
MOMENT

The Rebel Belle

Tuck Self

"If you obey all the rules, you miss all the fun." – *K. Hepburn*

I am "rebeliciously" excited to lift my skirt, show a li'l bit of my petticoat ruffle, and reveal my journey from southern belle to Rebel Belle.

Have I always been this bold? Absolutely not. I was taught that it is conceited and arrogant to love myself out loud, to talk about my life or toot my own horn. Me, a rebel? Me, a rule-breaker? Not a chance!

Born in the 1950s in a small southern town, I was schooled in the rules of genteel southern behavior. My mother insisted upon all the social graces. She raised me to be small, quiet, and polite; to stay in my place, act pretty, and speak when spoken to. Never was I to speak my truth, especially around men or other people of authority. Instead, I was taught to nurture the needs of others at the expense of my own freedom and happiness.

Tapping into the innate grace and charm characteristic of southern women, I learned to play the game very early. I became a chameleon, shifting roles from moment to moment. It didn't matter what I wanted to be: I was what was expected of me, and I was equipped to do it all. I was in awe of my mother, who was like Katie Scarlett O'Hara's twin sister. I dressed in her clothes, shoes and hats. I daintily drank coffee and smoked my candy cigarettes. I hosted tea parties and bridge clubs just like my mother and her southern sisters. I modeled these southern women of character who were nurturing and subservient, but also strong and powerful from holding families together during the war. With their guidance, I emerged quite successfully as a perfect southern belle.

But by the time I hit my forties, I was exhausted, and totally confused about my identity. Was I to ban the bra and make my place in the world, or keep the home fires burning? Was I the Perfect Daughter, the Junior League Socialite, the Career Woman, the Stay-at-Home Mom, or The Good Wife? Or was I none of these things? Who was this perfect li'l southern belle with the perfect southern lifestyle?

These questions began to stir a part of me that had been silent for years—a part of me that longed to rebel, resist, and push against the world. My inner Rebel Belle began speaking to me, softly at first, but then she began to rumble and roar.

The first step came when, after fifteen years as The Successful Career Woman, I asked my then-husband for permission to be The Stay-at-Home Mom. I decided I was tired of dressing up each day to look successful while entrusting my children to someone else's care. After all, that wasn't how my southern role models had done it.

Permission was granted, and I immersed myself in the country club scene, the social clubs, and the church groups. I car-pooled my children to dance, scouts, baseball, and soccer, just like my southern role models. I was free to live my Perfect Southern Life, and I thought I had it all. But as time went on, I found myself pondering how I dressed, how I decorated my home, how I interacted with my husband. How I was raising my children to live life the way I lived it: racing along in a quest to achieve, possess, and accomplish.

And then, one day, I came to a screeching halt and said to myself...

"Oh My God—I've finally become my mother!"

I don't remember being angry or frustrated by my epiphany, simply dumbfounded. I was in a Twilight Zone. I laugh about it now, but in that juicy, surreal moment I asked myself the question which should have been obvious all along: "If I'm not my mother, then *who am I?"*

That question spurred an internal revolution which liberated my Rebel Belle. That li'l voice I'd squashed and silenced for years suddenly couldn't wait to break free. For the first time, I unleashed my "rebelicious" spirit, and I gave myself permission to be me—whoever I was.

I reveled in my newfound freedom, learning and exploring. This new person was pretty interesting, I discovered. But one day that freedom took me a little too far. The perfect southern belle who'd always lived by the rules found herself in the middle of a love affair.

10

I was shocked at myself, and full of guilt. I wanted to die. I started to question my integrity, my spirit, my ability to be a good mother—even my right to be a parent and partner. By southern standards, I had made the biggest mistake of my life. In trying to rediscover myself, I had squandered my freedom. What would I do? Where would I go? How would I live? Would my family leave me? What would everyone think of me?

What did *I* think of me?

This, the most traumatic moment of my life, also became the most transformative moment of my life. I knew I had to be bold, honor my feelings, and tell the truth. I had to take responsibility and move forward. I couldn't make anyone wrong, not even me. I had to embrace the uncertainty of what was to come, and own my Rebel Belle.

Realizing that I needed support, I enrolled in counseling for the sixth time. My counselor instructed me to purchase a book called *The Seven Spiritual Laws of Success* by Deepak Chopra. For the first time ever, I was introduced to a concept called "life purpose." It gave me hope and direction, and compelled me to follow my heart, live my purpose, and make my mark on the world boldly, uniquely, and on my terms.

The book also taught me to embrace uncertainty. I was getting ready to leave my marriage, and I had no idea how I was going to take care of myself. But I knew that if I followed my heart and purpose, expressed my truth, and trusted my inner power, I would be upheld.

In my boldest self-expression yet, I announced my newfound freedom to my now ex-husband and left twenty years of The Perfect Southern Lifestyle behind. It was scary at first, but I trusted my heart. Children in tow, I set out on my own, firmly believing that, "When Mama is happy, everyone is happy." Owning my power and sharing my truth was a powerful thing. It freed the energy for all of us to heal.

That tumultuous period of my life was where I did my best work. I realize now that there was never anything to push or rebel against, only the opportunity to wake up to my truth and own my Rebel Belle. Today, I have an amazing life, amazing children, and an amazing relationship with my ex-husband. All of these things were built on the foundations of freedom, truth, and bold self-expression. When that nagging li'l voice inside says, "Who do you think you are? You're selfish. You'll never make it on your own!" my inner rebel continues to stand true, inspiring me to trust my voice and live on my terms.

Today, as I grab my petticoat ruffles, lift my skirt, and high-step my way through my fabulous southern life, I embrace my roots and all of the roles I've played. I'm one big, bold, "rebelicious" package of all my juicy experiences. I am the child of an alcoholic and a child of divorce. I was raised by a single mom and an absentee dad. I have been rich, and I have been poor. I have been loved by my girlfriends and ostracized by these same girlfriends. I have excelled in team sports and solo sports. I have been married and divorced. I have been a single mom, and I have been an empty-nester. I have been a Christian, a Jesus freak, and a child of the Universe. I have been overweight, and I have been anorexic. I have experienced infidelity, and I have experienced the love of a soul mate. I have worked successfully in the corporate world, and out of my home. I have been an accountant, a personal trainer, a network marketer, and, finally, a solo business owner and life coach. I have experienced the love and the deaths of a best friend, a boyfriend, and my parents. I am a sister, and a proud mom.

And finally...

I am a woman loving life, embracing my roles, transforming my fears, and looking for what blows my skirt up. (That's southern slang for "what rocks my world!") Step by step, I'm learning who I am and what I am here to do, and I'm having fun along the way. I'm proud to toot my own horn, and boldly proclaim to the world: I'm a southern belle living a "rebelicious" life—full out, on my terms.

Toot, toot!

Juicy Questions

Does this story speak to you? The journaling prompts below can help you access messages from your authentic core, and integrate the richness and insights of this story into your own juicy, joyful life!

Do the conventions of society or family play a major role in how you express yourself?

_____

_____

_____

_____

Has adhering to these conventions benefitted or hindered you in your personal growth?

_____

_____

_____

_____

If these conventions did not exist, what would your life look like? Who would you be?

_____

_____

_____

_____

Chasing Nuns

Ellie Bassick-Trovato

My husband's blue eyes crinkled as he watched our son giggle and flirt his way into the good graces of the nun at the next table. We touched fingers under the table, too far apart to really hold hands, but close enough to let each other know we were there. Ben, our two-year-old pocket full of blond sunshine, squirmed in his high chair, craning his neck to meet the gaze of the adoring nun.

We glanced up when we felt movement at the next table; Ben's bright smile faded. The nun was rising from her seat. Diminutive and regal, she proffered her good-byes to her companions and, offering Ben one last smile, made her way to the door.

Suddenly, John and I locked eyes, the same thought flipping our hearts in unison.

I broke the silence first, "A nun! We don't have a nun praying for you!"

"I know! Go! Stop her!" He laughed his throaty, from-the-belly chuckle, giddy with the possibilities that having a nun on our side would bring.

Every nerve in me twitched, aching to go—but still, I hesitated, looking from Ben to John. Ever since his first bloody, terrifying seizure with Ben on the changing table, we had decided that John shouldn't be left in sole charge of Ben. But we were in a restaurant! There were lots of people around who would help if something happened. I scanned the table for possible red flags, but didn't see how my two boys could possibly be in danger if I was back in five minutes.

Then, I flew.

As I jumped up from the table, I caught the comical round "O" Ben's mouth made, and the befuddled concern that furrowed his brows. And I, who was always careful to help Ben understand what was going on around him because there was so much he couldn't control— I just ran. I nearly knocked over a small child toddling through the door of the restaurant on shaky colt legs.

Outside, the late summer sun shimmered off hundreds of cars. Shielding my eyes, I scanned the parking lot shared by the 99 Restaurant, our local supermarket, and Blockbuster. At last, I caught a glimpse of a petite, hunched figure stopping near a silver car, and bellowed across the heads of the people moving toward the restaurant entrance, "Excuse me!"

The nun stopped. Well, really, everybody did.

The world around us froze in a blurred rainbow of colors as I ran to her, gasping and breathless.

"I'm so sorry to be rude, but do you remember the little boy you smiled at in there?"

Her quick smile and ready, "Of course!" was all the encouragement I needed. "He's my son," I told her, "and the man with us is my husband, John. He's been diagnosed with a brain tumor the size of a grapefruit. They say he won't make it, but we know he can. We have so many people praying for him, but I don't think we have an actual nun. Would you be kind enough to pray for him? Please?"

I was only half aware that I sounded utterly crazy. Possibly I was saying something insulting or rude; I didn't care. I had left a stream of open-mouthed onlookers in my wake. That hadn't phased me either.

In that moment, my transformation was complete. I chose to embrace love in its many radiant forms—hope, faith, joy, possibility, and determination—and knew that I would move heaven and earth in my single-minded quest to deny the outcome decreed by the doctors. I let go of the endless and exhausting dance of worry and fear-based "what-ifs," and let my desire for action propel me forward in such a way that there was no room for worry or fear, only the pure intention of asking the nun to provide us one more line to God's ear.

In that instant, I took a giant leap into a philosophy from which I have not veered since. From that moment on, I would honor the voice of love as the highest good, and be firm in my belief in a higher power that is all and only about love. Chasing that nun through the parking

16

lot crystallized for me the importance of faith, of believing something with my heart I couldn't know with my mind. No matter how many bumps and bruises I would suffer on my life's journey, I realized that I could choose to look for the gifts. Gifts like the nun sitting in the booth next to ours, or family rifts mended in the wake of John's diagnosis. Gifts like a little boy's blue eyes that mirrored his daddy's.

Religion to me had always been like a wool sweater: beloved because it once kept my dad warm, but itchy and uncomfortable when I actually put it on. Some ideas offered solace and comfort, but others felt raw and confining. I could never fully embrace the idea of a higher power who would judge so harshly those who strayed from a narrow idea of what was right. But in the moment when I burst out the door of the 99 Restaurant in search of the Holy Grail nun, I finally found a God who fit me comfortably in every way.

My God is a philosophy, not a narrowly defined archetype scripted by men in robes. My God is a God who smiles on the sweet, fervent daughter of a friend who called every night to pray like a banshee; a God who embraces the people who performed Reiki on John every week, and in doing so became part of our family. My God is the God who led me to the amazing man I called my husband, and to the sweet and noble nun in the parking lot. My God is a God who blesses those like Maureen Hancock, the gifted medium who, by relaying irrefutable messages from John's friend who had recently passed, proved beyond doubt that even in death our loved ones are still with us. My God is a God of love, not of retribution, and offers me abundant opportunities to define and discover who I am, and of what exactly I am made.

I couldn't know it then, but the biggest challenge to my new philosophy lay months ahead, in the twists and turns our lives took as my husband's sparkling eyes gradually faded into vacancy through hospital trips, MRIs, seizures, medication, and surgery. It became harder—and all the more important—to look through the lens of faith, love, and gratitude. I focused on the love of neighbors, friends, and family who shoveled our walkways, bought our groceries, and helped us pay our mortgage. I focused on bringing John every experience he wanted to have before his death. Through the generosity of friends and strangers, he was able to take Ben on his first trip to a frosty Fenway Park; it was surreal, with the bleachers buried under a foot of snow, and a half dozen frozen seagulls perched atop the Green Monster. I also helped him say goodbye to those he loved with bear totems to represent his fierce and loyal love, a reminder that he would always watch over them.

I miss my husband's twinkly blue eyes, but I am forever grateful for the lessons I learned in loving—and losing—him. It would appear, on one level, that our prayers were not answered, but I know they were. We prayed for safe passage, and for our best and highest good, and although it takes an immense leap of faith to believe it, we got these things. I may never fully understand *why* or *how* what happened was for our highest good, but that simply doesn't change my faith that it was.

My father passed away two months before my husband. My heart was heavy that winter, and yet, those experiences of loss held tremendous gifts. When these two cherished men let go of their lives, they gave me a stronger, richer version of mine. The two most devastating events of my life taught me that nothing can devastate me. I evolved from a woman who had struggled with depression for twenty years to a woman who has the strength and courage to move mountains.

From those darkest hours, I emerged with an unshakable belief that something bigger than us is in charge. My new relationship with that higher power enfolds me like a warm blanket of peace. My faith is rewarded every few months with an undeniable message through a medium from my dad or John. It turns out they are around me often, loving me still. John recently relayed what I was wearing when I found his old fishing rods—now even more precious, since a new man in my life taught Ben how to fish. Ben's face when he caught his first fish: pure delight. Ben's face when he discovered he'd be able to fish with his dad's fishing rod: pure pride.

Today, when I look in Ben's seven-year-wise blue eyes, the mirror image of his dad's, I am reminded that I am blessed. Not only did I have a chance to know shimmering, soul-stirring love, I have been blessed to learn that life is exactly—and only—what I make of it. The choice I have every day is the choice we all have: whether to look at life's challenges through the lens of fear, or the lens of love.

I choose love.

Juicy Questions

Does this story speak to you? The journaling prompts below can help you access messages from your authentic core, and integrate the richness and insights of this story into your own juicy, joyful life!

Looking back on a challenge or loss in your life, can you describe three good things that came from it?

_____

_____

_____

_____

Have you ever stepped across a threshold which significantly changed the way you view your life or your faith?

_____

_____

_____

_____

Identify something in your life that you fear. How would this challenge look if you viewed it through the lens of love?

_____

_____

_____

_____

Storms, Still Points, and Angels: A Modern Fairy Tale

Rev. Nina Roe

"...And the good little angel lived happily ever after."

Oh wait, let me start over, because the part before that is the juiciest. That's the part where I have my first earth shattering, life changing, mind blowing still point. I admit, it feels like so many lifetimes ago that it's somewhat clouded in mist, like a fairy tale. But it's a true story.

In case you're wondering, a still point is a moment in time when everything stops. Events leading up to the still point have primed the pump for a major shift to occur—a perfect storm, if you will. Then, in the eye of the storm, that tiny space of seconds, the absence of movement allows for unparalleled clarity, culminating in the unforgettable "Ah-ha!"—when you feel with every cell of your being that things are different, and that there's no going back.

And now, on with our story...

Once upon a time, a perfect storm was brewing. The year was 1998. The place: Massachusetts, U.S.A. I was a Vice President in systems development for a large financial firm in Boston. The technology boom during the early '90s had fueled enormous growth, and we'd hired accordingly—but that fall, when the stock market took a turn and the economy slowed, we were forced to lay off large numbers of staff, about a third of whom were from my group.

As it turned out, my boss was part of the cutbacks, so now I was reporting to a new guy. He and I were about as different as Gandhi and a drill sergeant. He took structure and hierarchy to a whole new level. He was in the office by 7:00 a.m., went running at lunch, and stayed until at least 6:00 p.m., unless it was Friday. The expected photo of his wife and two kids was strategically placed on his well-organized desk.

Instead of artwork, he hung plaques and certificates of achievement dating back to his days in the military. His success came from his belief that work is not a place for fun; it's a place for work. Hey, that was cool—it obviously worked for him.

I, on the other hand, had done well with a very different approach. As the mother of two small children, my days were anything but predictable. Every other week, I travelled to Dallas, where half of my staff was located. On the days I wasn't travelling, I would do the morning routine and work late if my husband Peter had an early meeting; otherwise, I would come in on the first train and leave at 4:00 p.m. for the afternoon mommy-shift. If one of my cherubs woke up vomiting, well...Peter and I had long since mastered the art of parenting in the moment.

Organization? I inherited my abilities in this area from my father, who invented his own method of filing: piles. (Oddly, we always seem to know where things are.) As for office art, one of the perks of my last promotion was an invitation to browse the firm's private gallery. I chose two prints featuring sheep, which went quite nicely with my sizable selection of crayon drawings by my young children.

I was not scheduled. I was not regimented. I brought family and fun into the workplace. And I was really good at what I did.

I loved my job for twelve years, but it had changed—a lot. My staff had been cut by a third and I was working for a man who had no idea why I would want pictures of sheep on my walls. The gloom that hung over the entire company was palpable. I recall walking through the corridors, hearing a voice crying "Poison! Poison! Get out!" It sounded like the robot from that old TV show, *Lost in Space*, frantically shouting, "Danger Will Robinson!" I now know this to be one of my first clear angel moments.

And so, the stage was set, all the elements had been summoned, and the seas were running high in front of my perfect storm. Then, along came the holiday season.

After the memories of Thanksgiving had faded, my son Theron was helping me to hang the stockings in our front hall—their holding area before the proper hanging over the fireplace on December 24th.

Together, we took out our four stockings. I asked him to hand them to me one by one. As we were cheerfully humming Christmas songs, Theron asked, "Mommy? How come there are four stockings?"

"Because there are four people in our family," I replied. "Why? How many do you think there should be?"

"Three."

"Really? Three? There's you, your sister, Daddy and me. Who aren't you counting?"

He looked up at me with his pure blue, loving eyes. "You, Mommy," he told me. "Because you're never around."

There it was: my still point. I honestly don't remember what I said next. I was in a state of shock. In that tiny space of a moment, my world was rocked, and there was no going back.

Later that evening, I told Peter what had happened, and that I felt it was time for me to leave my job. He had a good job, but we'd sacrificed in the interest of my career because I had greater potential at my company. As I was earning well over six figures, leaving my job meant a significant reduction in our family's income, at least temporarily. There wasn't much discussion, however, because on some level, we both knew there was no choice.

I gave my notice the next day.

I did the mommy thing, the school committee thing, and the carpool routine. Financially, we found ways to manage. I think back to that initial fear, and ponder the obstacles the ego is capable of constructing when it really wants to. We were always going to be okay; we just had to trust that we would.

Eventually, my angels tapped me on the shoulder once again. "It's time," they whispered.

I experienced another still point moment in a dowsing class. Dowsing rods (also known as divining rods) move with the energy around you in response to your intention. Discovering that I could use these tools to communicate with loving spirits was a huge revelation. That day, I learned that angels really exist, and that I can talk to them!

And so I tumbled down the rabbit hole, slipping into a world where only love, compassion and delight had a place. I discovered

23

that if I surrender and let my angels lead the way, magic happens. They guide me with everything—from little choices like what to eat or how to dress, to bigger choices involving career, health, and relationships.

There are a million examples I could share about how the angels enrich my life, but this one is pure girly fun. About a month ago, the angels insisted I stop at Pier One. I happened to have a coupon for a discount if I spent over $150, though I had no intention of buying that much. As soon as I walked into the store, my body was gently pulled to one area; then, I heard them whisper, "Behind you!" I turned around and saw a chair with a large sunflower on it—and it was on sale! Now, that may not seem like a big deal, but one of my best friends loves sunflowers, and her birthday happened to be two weeks away. I had no choice but to buy the chair.

That evening, I invited my friend to stop by our house on her way home from work. When she arrived, I told her to close her eyes. I led her to the chair. "This is the sunflower chair from Pier One, isn't it?" She laughed as she sat down. "I was in there last weekend and wanted to buy it, but my angels told me not to!" Needless to say, the angels once again batted a home run, and my friend was a very happy woman.

I experience doubt and discouragement just like every other human on this earth, but my perspective has shifted. I see purpose in all things. I witness deep, unbridled beauty. I own gratitude. I appreciate the still points, and ask what I can learn from the storms.

I have travelled beyond the dowsing rods and now teach angel communication, sharing my stories of a life lived in the company of angels. I've reclaimed an awareness that was all but lost prior to that still point initiated by my little boy. Now, my nest is emptying, and my path continues to evolve. I know without question that I am here in this lifetime to teach others that angels surround every moment of every day. I model my fairy tale lifestyle, and demonstrate that it is not something I was born with, but something that can be learned—that this kind of serenity is the birthright of every human being. We are all destined to live happily ever after!

Juicy Questions

Does this story speak to you? The journaling prompts below can help you access messages from your authentic core, and integrate the richness and insights of this story into your own juicy, joyful life!

Nina had to let go of something—in this case, her job—in order to allow something new and better to enter her life. What can you let go of to make room for what you truly want?

_____

_____

_____

_____

Do you believe that you have angels or spirit guides present beside you each day? If so, how can you connect more deeply with them?

_____

_____

_____

_____

Often, we don't hear the voices of our angels (spirit guides, higher selves) because our minds are too busy with other tasks. How can you make time to slow down your mind and listen?

_____

_____

_____

_____

You Too Will Bloom

Margery Phelps

At first I thought it was just a happy coincidence, but in the exquisite moment that followed my discovery, I realized there was a profound lesson for me, and that insight changed my life. But how could a fern in a shower stall be the agent of my rebirth and renewal?

It all started on Valentine's Day, when my brother-in-law gave me another lovely orchid. His yearly love offering to my indoor garden had become a tradition, and I now had four of the exotic plants. The purple phalaenopsis was the most beautiful and majestic yet, and stood in a place of honor on the sofa table, in front of a large window, where it could be admired from both indoors and out.

But alas, as always happens with orchids, the blooms faded and fell away a mere five or six months later, leaving sturdy, graceful leaves and a rather pathetic stem. No longer majestic, my phalaenopsis now looked lonely and barren.

By now, it was mid-summer, and the fern on my front porch was growing grandly, greeting visitors with long, fine-leafed fronds that seemed to reach out and touch them in welcome. It was by far the most beautiful fern I had ever raised, and it brought admiring comments from even the most discerning gardeners in my neighborhood.

Summer faded to fall, then fall to winter. Freezing weather meant my fern was doomed. I could not bear to lose my front-door greeter, so I toted her, still in her ample plant stand, upstairs to my master bathroom, where I gave her a winter home in the marble shower stall. Not wanting her to be lonely in her new living quarters, I placed the orchids on the lower shelf of the plant stand. They were all bedraggled and sad—a reflection of my own mental, spiritual, and physical condition. I didn't have to look at their misery, though: the long fronds of the fern hung almost to the shower floor, hiding them from view. Out of sight, out of mind.

At that point, I was not in a good place emotionally, and I felt lonely a great deal of the time. While recovering from a broken neck several years prior, I'd gained weight, and my self esteem fell through the floor. Why did that dynamic person I used to be go away? Where was she hiding? Where was the person who gave lectures on health and wellness—the person who once wrote a coloring book to make nutrition education for children a fun-loving adventure?

The dramatic fall that almost paralyzed me and left me with a useless right arm took away more than just my confidence. I was a writer: my right arm was my life. Writing was my passion. I found an indescribable joy and contentment in allowing the energy of the universe to flow into my mind, down my arm, and through my hand onto a piece of paper. It did not matter to me that no one ever read what I wrote. I wrote for my own pleasure and discovery; to resolve personal problems and conflicts, and to connect with my Source.

28 I underwent two surgeries to reconnect my arm to my body and my head to my neck, and endured three arduous years of rehabilitation. These eventually put me back in pretty good working order—but during that time I lived in four different residences, and lost touch with many friends. I seldom saw my children, not wanting them to think of me as a burden. I gave up writing and turned back to my accounting education to support myself as a bookkeeper and office management consultant.

I was wrung out spiritually and felt disconnected from God. I constantly wondered why my life had taken such an unpleasant turn. My only solace was my garden and my dog. Had it not been for the devotion and care of my twin sister Mary and her husband Jay, I probably would have given up completely.

Winter descended upon us with freezing rains and bone-chilling winds; my garden was gone, and the empty back patio off the kitchen was a bleak reminder that my life was not in season either. It had been five years since the accident, and I still did daily physical therapy. Would the life I had loved ever find its way back to me?

Thanksgiving and Christmas came and went. Tax season brought a flurry of client activity. And the fern, now accustomed to her weekly shower in the upstairs bath, grew and thrived and doubled in size. I began to wonder how I would ever move her back to the porch.

February 14th rolled around again, as did Jay with another orchid. With an elated flourish, I put it in the place of honor on the sofa table.

"How are the other orchids doing?" he asked.

After a long pause, during which I tried to remember what I had done with the expensive plants, I realized that they were still under the fern. "Oh, they're upstairs," I told him, trying to dismiss his inquiry. I was ashamed to admit that, like me, the orchids were hiding. They were no longer beautiful and blithe, doing something worthwhile with their lives. Instead, they were existing in a state of apathy, ugliness, and profound sadness.

During our Valentine's Day lunch, I couldn't help but think about the orchids. As soon as Jay dropped me off at my house, I ran upstairs to the shower. It had been months since I had laid eyes on them. Every week when I turned on the shower to water the fern, I told her how lovely and handsome she was—but there was never even a thought for the orchids, nor any kind words for them. How could I have been so cruel to any living organism?

With some trepidation, I pulled back the rich green fronds of the fern. The orchids were such a metaphor for my own life—in the distant past they had been beautiful and blooming. What had I done to them? What had been done to me?

What had I done to myself?

To my sheer delight and amazement, a beautiful purple phalaenopsis bloom smiled up at me. I was shocked. How could something so beautiful come out of such a sad situation? One by one, I retrieved the plants. Each one was either in full bloom or full of buds. I gingerly cleaned their pots, carried them downstairs, and put them on the sofa table.

In their darkest hour, when they were at their worst, my orchids were given refuge under a fern. Unbeknownst to me, the weekly showers of the fern had given the orchids the exact humidity they

29

needed to not only survive, but to thrive. While in hiding, they were being renewed, preparing to bloom again.

And bloom they did.

In that moment I understood that just as the fern was a safe haven for the orchids, God has been and always will be my sanctuary. In the darkest, ugliest hours of life, He is hanging over me, giving me what I need to not only survive, but to thrive. I have only to be willing to take refuge.

Now, I see life in a new way. Each challenge is an opportunity for rebirth; every storm is an agent of renewal. By focusing on the outcome—that I *will* bloom again—the dark hours are shorter, the storms gentler. In the shelter of the Almighty, I am never alone.

Juicy Questions

Does this story speak to you? The journaling prompts below can help you access messages from your authentic core, and integrate the richness and insights of this story into your own juicy, joyful life!

What mental, physical or emotional challenges have you faced in your life? How did they affect your view of yourself?

_____

_____

_____

_____

Many of us hide ourselves from the world in some way—whether from insecurity, fear, or (like Margery) the desire not to be a burden on others. How can you cultivate growth and renewal in your periods of solitude, rather than fear or bitterness?

_____

_____

_____

_____

Take a moment to plan your reemergence. What does your brightest bloom look like? How can you share your most beautiful self with the world?

_____

_____

_____

_____

DISCOVERING YOUR
Authentic SELF

The Message in the Mirror

Lynnet McKenzie

What do you see when you look in the mirror?

Most of my life, I could not look into a mirror without cringing. My eyes went instantly to the flaws in my reflection, dissecting and critiquing my body from head to toe. I saw myself as unattractive to the point of gross disfigurement. Even though I found the everyday women around me perfectly lovely and lovable as their natural selves, I held myself to an airbrushed standard I could never attain. I believed that if only I could be beautiful, I would be loved.

There were many causes for my twisted self-image. Recurrent sexual abuse, well-meaning but clueless parents, and an endless stream of messages from media combined to fuel the inner critic that kept me playing the victim. I lost touch with the power of my truth and intuition at an early age. Being a victim meant I always needed to be rescued, and my disconnection from my own power meant I always looked for rescue from something outside myself.

During the first few years of my life, things were very different for me. I was very connected to my intuitive powers, and had no thought of being unattractive. Until I turned five, seeing angelic beings and communing with trees was natural for me. In the realm of nature and spirit, I had no self-consciousness at all. When I entered school, however, the other children's reactions informed me that this was "freakish" behavior, so I closed the door to this connection.

I did not meet my intuitive self again until I was twenty-two, when I became seriously ill and learned I had large tumors in my uterus. The blessing in my desperation was that I began hearing spiritual messages again. These messages led to a metaphysical healing, which removed the tumors instantly.

Filled with a magic lost since my early childhood, I set out for a walk in the woods the very next day. My heart was wide open after my healing, but I was still surprised when I heard a large Douglas Fir on the edge of the trail call to me. I stopped and listened, choosing to believe what I was hearing rather than hurrying on my way.

As I opened fully to my connection with the tree, the ground suddenly felt sacred, so I removed my shoes and soaked in the sensation of the earth beneath my feet. I knew that whatever I wished for in that moment would manifest with great strength. So, I looked into the depth of my being and proclaimed my deepest, most heart-felt desire. In a voice filled with pain and longing, I said, "I want love!"

I was not pleased when the tree began laughing at me. Soon, the other trees all around joined in, creating a chorus of rustling laughter. To me, there was nothing funny about this at all. I wanted my pain to be taken seriously.

The grand Fir let me in on the joke. "Silly girl," it said. "You say you want love, but you *are* love. *You are love*!" Then it resumed its musical laughter. For a moment, I was stunned. "I *am* love?" I had been suffering and searching all these years. And now a tree in the forest tells me that I *am* the very thing I have been searching for? But then, I chose to let my heart receive the message, and I laughed too, finally understanding the joke.

I walked home barefoot, a little stunned, still chuckling to myself. When I arrived, I went straight to the bathroom to wash my dirty feet. I put one foot in the sink and glanced up at my reflection. Until this point, all I had ever seen of myself were my flaws. But in that moment of opening, I saw myself truly for the first time.

I was the most beautiful thing I had ever seen.

I saw the whole Universe in my eyes. I saw the beauty and magic of creation, both in my physical form, and in the light in my eyes that transcended form. I must have stood with one foot in the sink for twenty minutes, just staring at my reflection. For the first time ever, I loved what I saw in the mirror.

I'd like to say that I remained "awake" from this point forward, but the truth is that I did nothing to keep the awakening alive. After a week or two, I'd convinced myself that I had a seriously over-active imagination. Within months, I'd resumed my chronic self-abuse.

What followed was another sixteen years of chronic fatigue, anxiety, relationship issues, illnesses, and debilitating injuries. Even with all the wise teachings I had read and magnificent messages I had received, I still wanted someone or something outside myself to save me. In my highly educated ignorance, I kept myself imprisoned, waiting impatiently for rescue—until two years ago, when, at the age of thirty-eight, my neck was seriously injured in an auto accident, leaving me disabled and in constant, excruciating pain. The discs and vertebrae in my lower neck were damaged, and a bone spur was poking dangerously into my spinal cord. All the physical activity which had previously defined my life and career became impossible. Over the next year, I lost muscle tone and gained forty pounds of cushion. This was like pouring gasoline onto the smoldering embers of my self-loathing, My inner critic didn't just flare: she exploded.

And this was good. Finally, the emotional and physical pain became more than I could bear, and I *had* to take action. Even if I did not know how to love myself, I love my son enormously: for his sake, I could not let myself go down in flames. I returned to the mirror.

There are moments when we must stretch beyond our self-imposed limitations and reach for our bigger selves. Most of my life, I had been looking outward and asking, "When is my life going to change?" But this time, I asked a new question: "How must I change?"

Sometimes, in order to get the answer we're looking for, we just have to ask the right question.

It was then that I realized I had to transform my own thinking, and stop seeking a man or a miracle to make things better for me. It was time for me to "rescue" myself by making the choice to stop being a victim of my own mind. And the best part was that, on the other side of this choice, there was an amazing gift waiting for me: myself! There I was, in the mirror, a bit changed physically but still filled with the beauty of the Universe.

Over the previous twenty years, I had tried to improve my self-esteem with counseling, support groups, workshops, vision quests, and

37

a library of self-help books. None of these things produced the kind of shift that happened when I took responsibility for my own happiness. I chose to reconnect with the wise, intuitive voice inside myself, and stop listening to the screaming critic (whose voice becomes softer the longer I practice this). I chose to stop focusing on what is "wrong" with me, and focus instead on the beauty and joy within me.

And what a relief it is to take responsibility for loving myself and meeting my own needs! What a joy it is to be kind to myself! It has proved to be the foundation I was lacking for success in relationships, health, and business.

Choice is the greatest power we possess. Loving myself is a choice I make every time I look in the mirror. I do not need to be "beautiful enough" to be loved. I *am* love, and there is nothing more beautiful than that.

We all have the same power within ourselves, and the same choice to make. And we all have the same amount of time, which is always, ever, *now*.

Juicy Questions

Does this story speak to you? The journaling prompts below can help you access messages from your authentic core, and integrate the richness and insights of this story into your own juicy, joyful life!

Can you look in the mirror and love what you see, without judgment or conditions? If not, how can you treat yourself more lovingly?

_____

_____

_____

_____

Do you externalize your struggles? If you are waiting for something outside yourself to step in and make things better for you, how can you shift your thinking and take responsibility for your own happiness?

_____

_____

_____

_____

Lynnet desired love, and was told that she was love. Very often, the things we desire are already present in our lives. What do you most want? Where is it already present in your life, and how can you acknowledge and nurture it?

_____

_____

_____

_____

Into the Light

Caia Martin

"When you come to the edge of all the light you know,
and are about to step off into the darkness of the unknown,
faith is knowing one of two things will happen: there will be
something solid to stand on, or you will be taught how to fly."
— *Patrick Overton*

I 'll never forget the time I was lost—because it wasn't for a minute, or an hour, or a day, it was for years. My becoming lost was a slow process of not listening to my own inner voice, and instead following the advice of others. It stemmed from low self-esteem, and an idea that grew deep within me about not feeling loved and supported.

As a child, I honored and dutifully listened to the elders in my life. I worked hard to fulfill their expectations and subscribe to their visions, all the while feeling like no one truly understood me. I was a right brained, spiritual thinker who bubbled with imagination, loved art, and always dreamed *big*, but most of the people around me were left-brained, analytical thinkers who required facts and figures to operate their lives. Connection, creativity and inner voices didn't jibe with them, and since their world was the world I lived in, their rules were the rules I had to follow. Feeling like I was trapped in an environment that left little room for my own thoughts, I eventually grew weary of trying to make myself heard. By the age of fifteen, I found myself believing that everyone else must know better—and that was how I got lost.

I managed to stay true to my ideals through high school, even though my parents, fearing I would get lost elsewhere, sent me to a smaller, more traditional school, with a smaller, more traditional mindset. There, I learned to keep my thoughts quietly inside, living them in secret, no longer looking for outside support. But having no reference point, and no one to collaborate with, slowly stifled my inner voice, and by the time I finished college, I was no longer very good at hearing it. I often found myself ignoring, questioning, or rebelling against it until, like a pouting child, the voice finally stopped talking to me at all—or at least, I stopped listening. That was when my real descent into darkness began.

The decisions I made from that point on, although never life-threatening, were life-altering. I had unconsciously traded my carefree life for one of selective suffering and despair. I say "selective" because, in truth, many things in my life were going quite well. I had a fantastic job, I traveled, I had great friends—but my choices about men and love were ultimately devastating. I frequently chose narcissistic men whose controlling personalities and vapid ideology pulled me further and further from my core beliefs; men whose very existence in my life opened my world to pain, angst and strife.

My relationships went from bad to worse, and I eventually found myself isolated and alone as I struggled to survive in a failing marriage for the second time. Too embarrassed to admit that I was stuck in an abusive, soul-stealing relationship with a man I loathed, I weathered the neglect, abuse and despair—all the while trying to ignore a deep knowing that I was living life in direct opposition to who I really was.

Life in our house reached a fevered pitch as, for the first time ever, the abuse spread. I was no longer its only victim. My happy-go-lucky three-year-old son had run into it headlong. His father lashed out in actions and words that cut deeply, stealing away my beautiful boy's innocence and spirit in one fell swoop. The shock and horror of it was unfathomable to me—but more shocking was that at the same moment I found myself paralyzed, unable to intervene, or do anything more than sit helplessly in the absurdity of it.

Up until that point, I had honestly believed I could protect my children, that my love would shield them. But now, there was no denying it: I was powerless to stop him, and I couldn't protect us. Waves of despair swept through me—anger, disgust, and betrayal, followed by helplessness, self-loathing and hatred—each knocking me off my feet and thrashing me in their undertow until I could no longer bear the pain.

Days passed; I was empty and exhausted. Even thinking had become difficult. Then, late one night, as I sat rocking my brand new baby girl, the choices I had made caught up to me. I began sobbing uncontrollably, begging for support as the vastness of our situation enveloped me. I cried for hours, demanding help. "Anyone, someone, please, I'm lost. I don't know how to get out of this mess!"

I screamed, I cried. Then, in the spaces between my tears, I finally heard my inner voice speaking to me again, quietly but insistently urging me to take inventory of my life.

I did. I looked from every angle. I poured over truths and realities, searching desperately for ways to make sense of it. How had I gotten here? How had I become the opposite of who I wanted to be? My heart sank as I realized I wasn't strong, I was weak. I wasn't a hero, I was a victim.

Tears welled as my thoughts turned to my children. Who would I be if I let them grow up thinking this is what they should expect from life? When would this life take its toll on them, too? How could I let them grow up thinking I was weak, or believing that we had no power?

In that moment, something began to change. I could sense a resolve growing within me. "No one deserves this," I shouted at the darkness. "This is not healthy or right!" Courage infused my soul. "I will not let my children grow up believing this is how other people should treat them—or worse, that this is how they should treat others. No! This *will not be our life!*"

Something *had* changed. As I sat now in the quiet of my room, I could clearly hear my inner voice speaking to me again. With passion and steely determination, I bombarded it with questions, asking for guidance. I needed to get out. I needed to save my children and myself from the hell I had manifested for us. I pleaded and prayed, and slowly the answers came. I found strength in that voice—a friend, even. Bit by bit, I began to pull us out of the darkness and into a new life filled with hope and promise, with light and not dark; a life where I began to see that anything was possible, once I learned to ask and listen.

My life changed on the day I began to listen to my inner voice again. Throughout my divorce I was able to stand strong, steadfast in my resolve that nothing less than everything I wanted was acceptable to me anymore. The life I have now is rich and abundant. There is laughter, love and joy. My children and I, although still works in progress, are happy and healthy.

Looking back, I am thankful for having been lost. There was tremendous value in traveling that road, and the experiences I had along the way have given me contrast and perspective, taught me to be strong, and helped me understand the value of trusting in who I am—authentically, at my core.

We all have our own journeys to take, and I encourage you to embrace yours. But first things first: make sure to pack your inner voice! It is the best compass you will ever find, and it will lead you where you want to go. While you're at it, don't forget to load up your bag with passion. Fill it with what you believe in—your ideals, your values, the things that drive you—then, set your course for your brave, bold new life, and start walking!

Juicy Questions

Does this story speak to you? The journaling prompts below can help you access messages from your authentic core, and integrate the richness and insights of this story into your own juicy, joyful life!

Do you feel that you are living authentically, in agreement with your ideals?

_____

_____

_____

_____

Caia speaks about being "lost." Have you ever felt as though you were disconnected from your authentic self? Do you listen closely to your inner voice, or do you squelch it in favor of what's easier, less frightening, or more popular?

_____

_____

_____

_____

What do you really want from your life? What is no longer acceptable to you?

_____

_____

_____

_____

Truly B, Truly Me

Kati Verburg

"Today you are you, it is truer than true. There is no one alive who is you-er than you." – *Dr. Seuss*

The better part of my childhood was filled with lovely sentiments such as the one above, as my parents reiterated to me and my siblings that our individuality made each of us special, one of a kind. While today, at thirty-eight, I understand these well-intended messages, it wasn't always so. For the better part of my life, I shied away from embracing my Me-ness because I just didn't like who I was. Instead, I gave my feelings of inadequacy permission to determine the course of my life.

There was a time—quite recently, in fact—when I would rather have stuck a fork in my eye than admit the error in my thinking. I preferred to cling tightly to my victimization.

Humility? What was that? Looking inward would require a great deal of it, and I was keenly aware that taking responsibility for my life meant much more than mere admission of the part I played in the outcome. It required change, and I continually allowed my lack of self-esteem to keep me from making any.

Like most people, I walked the treadmill of life, running to stand still, gaining little momentum on an arduous journey. I lacked real, unabashed joy, and instead carried around "oldies"—negative events from days gone by that rattled about in my brain. I delighted in reminding myself of my failures, calling to my consciousness things that served only to hurt me. I recalled my promiscuity in my teenage years, and pummeled my character for choices that I had no way of changing. I gave power to an abusive boyfriend I'd dumped long ago by allowing his degrading words about my body to continue to define the way I felt about the skin I lived in. I put myself down for leaving high school early, attaching "dropout"—and all that title presumes—to my psyche.

Yes, the better part of my trials stemmed from one very monumental fact: I hated myself. I hated my Me-ness, my one-of-a-kindness, and saw myself as little more than a stupid, fat slut. My self-esteem was in the toilet. Although my body took the brunt of my anger over the years, as I engaged in a brutal daily regimen of critical self-conduct in front of the mirror, the disgust I felt trickled down, affecting every last morsel of my belief in myself. I continually reminded myself that I was a bad wife, mother, daughter, sister, friend, cook, writer, bill-payer, lover, and neighbor.

I might have kept running on my treadmill of negativity, but my mother's death in 2005 triggered a grueling journey of introspection which permanently altered my thinking. I locked myself in my bedroom, redirecting my grief at the loss of my mother into anguish about myself, a process to which my negative self-esteem was a ready accomplice. Night after night, I whipped myself for whatever failure I could find lying around the recesses of my brain.

During those months, I quarantined myself in my bedroom for days on end, dissecting my integrity—much like I had once split a pigeon down the middle in my eighth grade Biology class to hunt for clues about what its last meal had been. I remember the pigeon's white wings were spread out wide and pinned to a tray, its head twisted sideways and its black eyes glazed over like a Krispy Kreme donut. I poked its foreign organs with my scalpel gingerly, as though they were asleep, and might suddenly fly up and out of the bird itself.

I saw myself as that same pigeon, lying on my back, wings pinned at my sides so that my insides might be rummaged through. I lay splayed open, unable to hide a single thing, totally vulnerable. But if I was the pigeon, I also was that burgeoning scientist, rummaging through the insides of the bird, half disgusted, half intrigued. What had my last meal been, I wondered. What had I been feeding myself?

What I discovered was that while I could trace my self-esteem issues to my teens, over the years I had become stunted. Now, I allowed the past events to dictate my life, believing that I was destined for nothing better than what I had already become: an angry, bitter woman with few aspirations but a lot of regrets. Victimization and blame had become close friends over the years, as I fueled my hatred for myself by reliving the stories of my past. In my mind, I revisited the sexual assault I endured at age twelve, vacillating between blaming myself and feeling sorry for myself. I reread journals from my mid-twenties that detailed my life as an anorexic, and felt sickened by both my disease and my weak state of mind, which nudged me toward that behavior again. I pushed my family away, feeling inadequate and broken compared to my siblings and the person my parents had hoped I would become.

Several months into my self-deprecating onslaught, my father sent me an e-mail related to chemical addictions. My initial thoughts were of drugs and alcohol, neither of which I was struggling with, and so I felt little need to read the article. His note, however, full of encouraging words and love, prompted me to open the attachment. When I did, I learned something absolutely astounding: emotions *are* addictions, governed by the same chemical process as drug addictions. As we repeat thoughts or emotions, our brains create long-term relationships in a neural network, making these feelings easier and easier to call on, and keeping us rooted in our past. When it comes down to it, our bodies are simply releasing signals to our brains to feed the monkeys on our backs.

While my negative experiences may have been real, and traumatic, and while each had a major impact on me, they only told the story of my past—not of my present, and certainly not of my future. The future, I came to realize, was up to me, and became changeable in my own mind the moment I decided to choose my thoughts and emotions. The only person with the ability to control whether or not I berated myself, whether I continued to seek out (and find) what was wrong with me, whether I continued to mutilate my fragile confidence and keep my wings pinned to my sides, was *me*. I saw that I had carried my old beliefs into adulthood, and that I'd wasted years poking and stabbing at my self-worth. I had choices about how I wished to treat myself, and I was continually choosing things that did not serve me.

I started my mental makeover with my body—overwhelmingly the biggest target of my psyche. Instead of engaging in my daily self-

49

deprecating behavior, I began to search out my best features in the mirror, deliberately overlooking my supposed "flaws." With a bit of patience and a whole lot of reprogramming, I came to find something beautiful in me, desirable even.

No longer did I see the freckled fatty with rocks-in-socks breasts, "Hello Betty" arm flab, and a pooter belly (known also by several less affectionate monikers). Instead, I came to see the icy blue eyes I inherited from my mother, the diamond-shaped chin I had drawn from my father, and the pale Irish skin I had received from both. I saw my curvaceous, womanly body. The pale, squiggly scars on my belly that spoke of skin stretched and pulled tight, I chose to view as badges of valor, a sign that I had brought two beautiful lives into this world.

Finally, I had taken control of the demon that had haunted me for the better part of my life, and relinquished blame and victimization. The fact that I could change something that was so deeply ingrained in my consciousness, something I had built an identity around—in essence, an addiction—that was *big*. After that, I could do anything.

This vast "Ah-ha!" moment brought about a personal awareness that was profound, and resulted in face-to-face, getting-to-know-you time with Me. It wasn't long before other aspects of my life were affected, as my attentiveness rippled outward. My relationships, my work, and practically any pursuit I became engaged in seemed to thrive as I set out to find the good in each, as opposed to fixating on the bad.

Today, in my awareness and resolution, I stand taller, secure in who I am and what I am capable of. I have come to respect my successes, and forgive my supposed failures. My long journey has finally brought me here, to a place of self-acceptance and even approval. I have finally embraced my Me-ness.

In a roundabout way, I have my mother to thank for my insights, for the loss of her brought me to a place of deep personal perspective. But, in the end, it was I who made the change—or, more accurately, the choice—to forgive myself, let the "oldies" go, and seek out the many amazing qualities I possessed all along. The good Doctor had it right, it is truer than true; there is no-one *you*-er than you!

Juicy Questions

Does this story speak to you? The journaling prompts below can help you access messages from your authentic core, and integrate the richness and insights of this story into your own juicy, joyful life!

What are your "oldies?" How do they keep you from embracing your You-ness?

_____

_____

_____

_____

Body image issues were a major problem for Kati. When you look in the mirror, can you see the beautiful woman staring back—or do you see only flaws?

_____

_____

_____

_____

Do you make conscious choices about how you treat yourself, or do you fall back on old habits and conditioning? How can you choose to treat yourself more compassionately?

_____

_____

_____

_____

Rock Your Goddess

Shann Vander Leek

Fresh from a delightful bubble bath, I admire my healthy form and thank the Universe that I've learned to embrace the Divine Feminine and love my body. I love my Shann-ness: curvaceous, soft, athletic and strong. It feels good to be at home with my inner Goddess.

I wasn't always this tuned in. I spent years bumping around with very little body-mind awareness. The disconnect was created by overindulging in my former high-stress career, participating in pointless drama, consistently eating high-calorie meals, and partying like a rock star with friends on the weekends.

I was also lost in my ego's aspirations. Always a chameleon, I blended into the predominately male management culture in which I was immersed. I played golf, drank good wine, and grew quite fond of fine restaurants. I loved earning piles of money, and I loved having the freedom to buy whatever I desired. I realize now that not only could I be quite arrogant on occasion, I was totally closed off to my own woman-hood. Playing a man's game in a man's world, it never occurred to me that I should flaunt the bright, creative, and soulful woman inside of me.

I spent years working at my high-pressure job during the day, and hanging out watching mind-numbing television at night. I had become physically inactive, with the exception of occasional walks and "weekend warrior" activities. My escalating body weight and over-the-top headaches finally got my attention: I'd kicked my body to the curb, and was completely out of touch with myself. I had to do something.

I took an inventory of my lifestyle choices, and made it a priority to find a new way of being. I learned how to take better care of myself in order to be fully present. Motherhood, combined with my newfound interest in personal development, helped me walk away from my career and a lifestyle that no longer suited me.

My personal recipe to rock my inner Goddess involves devoting time and energy to creating—and enjoying—a luscious life. Now, instead of feeling arrogant and out-of-touch, I find myself overflowing with creativity, loving kindness, and joy. I have learned how to combine creative expression, yoga, bodywork, positive self-talk, curiosity, natural beauty, and prayer into a "soul stew" that nourishes me inside and out.

My first step toward freeing the inner Goddess involved creating a delicious, comfortable and feminine environment. I adorned my walls with pleasing art and personal photographs. I created a bookshelf altar to showcase a few personal items including Petoskey stones, images of my family, candles, and a small statue of Kuan Yin. Fresh flowers have become part of my living space year round.

Occasionally, I will I spray lavender aromatherapy mist for a calming effect, or lemongrass to wake up my senses. Burning incense is a soothing ritual for mindfulness meditation, and an easy way to freshen a stale room.

I learned to reignite my creativity with vision boards and inspirational collages which represent my immediate desires. Choosing the images and crafting each project is a lot of fun. My daughter and I make collages several times each year. My current collage is filled with images of spring flowers, a dragonfly, the tail of a beautiful whale shooting out of the water, a long and winding road, and the gorgeous coastline of northern Kauai. I also included words and phrases like "Adventure," "Cutting Loose," "A Force of Nature," "Joyful Wisdom," and "Peace in oneself, peace in the world."

I honor my body with regular massage therapy. For me, receiving a massage is not a luxury, but a feminine obligation. In order to be my best self, I need to create time for healing and transformational bodywork. (In case you didn't know, massage therapy also lowers stress, promotes deep relaxation, and improves circulation!) I am blessed to have a great relationship with one of the best massage therapists on the planet.

Part of rocking my Goddess includes enjoying hot baths several times each week. I tend to bathe in the evening after I've tucked my daughter into bed. I love soaking in the calming, lighthearted energy of a bubble bath. Before I step in, I create a divine space complete with tea lights, incense, soothing music, and maybe a good book to read. A long and luxurious soak before bed helps me sleep more soundly.

From the time I took my first relaxing breath in Śavasana, I have been hooked on yoga. When I started practicing and teaching yoga and luscious living play-shops, I became filled with more loving kindness and humor than ever. Yoga helps me get in touch with myself on a deeper level, and nourishes my body-mind. I've learned to be gentle with myself through restorative poses, tuning into my breath, and noticing how I feel while moving my body.

Positive self-talk is my magic weapon against masochistic mental commentary. My ego-mind can be an unruly playground filled with bullies, tattletales, and monsters. When I am feeling small and emotionally drained, I tell myself, "I am enough. I am worthy. I am loved." When I am feeling battered by the inner bully, I acknowledge the feeling, and then ask the question, "Is this real?" Positive self-talk is a big part of my newly created feminine confidence. I am no longer willing to live in a guilt-ridden shame pit created by the "shoulds" of my ego. I realize now that I deserve serious self-care and unconditional self-love.

As a transition coach, I am constantly plugged into my computer and mobile phone, communicating with and supporting women every day. If I want to remain healthy and able to do my best work, it's essential for me to unplug from my highly-connected virtual environment. I create time each day to get out into the natural world. When I commit to hiking along a woodland trail or beachcombing on Lake Michigan, I improve my focus. When I feel overwhelmed by a stack of tasks, responsibilities, and commitments, I make it a priority to step away from the madness and soak up a little sweetness.

Igniting the magical flames of my curiosity has led me to many rich, engaging, and colorful new adventures. To be delightfully curious is refreshing; I am grateful to my daughter for helping me remember what child-like wonder feels like. There is no time like the present to act on something you have always wondered about!

Tuning into my higher power through prayer and meditation allows me to explore an expansive vision of my juicy, joyful life. I understand that I can face anything, as long as I make time to think through my current situation objectively, and allow the answers to each obstacle or challenge to unfold naturally. I am learning to be at peace with myself, my family and my community.

Not too long ago, my inner Goddess was boxed into a basement closet, crying out for attention. Now, she's sparkling every day in the full light of the sun. I am so grateful that I learned how to make self-care a priority. I adore every experience of allowing my Divine Feminine to unfold. I know now that I deserve to honor myself as woman, and I can't wait to unearth more shiny secrets as I continue to learn how to rock my Goddess!

Juicy Questions

Does this story speak to you? The journaling prompts below can help you access messages from your authentic core, and integrate the richness and insights of this story into your own juicy, joyful life!

How do you honor and celebrate your own femininity?

_____

_____

_____

_____

Is something in your life—like a job, a relationship, or the bully on your own mental playground—stifling your inner Goddess? If so, how can you implement positive change and let your Goddess shine?

_____

_____

_____

_____

When she's feeling drained, Shann tells herself, "I am enough. I am worthy. I am loved." What does your positive self-talk sound like? What does your inner Goddess need to hear?

_____

_____

_____

_____

LEARNING TO *Love* YOURSELF

Bring It On!

Cynthia deWet

Let me introduce myself. I am the beautiful, adorable, fun-loving, gifted, intuitive, lonely, forgotten child of an alcoholic father and a broken family.

I was a surprise that made my father march to the local bar for another drink, a surprise that caused my mother to delay leaving an unhappy marriage. I never realized there was a problem between my parents until my mother woke me one night from a deep sleep, and said, "Cindi, wake up! Your father and I are getting a divorce." I was twelve years old, and that was the beginning of my nightmare.

Prior to that night, I'd had no idea that there was anything wrong with our lives. I began to have a hard time trusting my perception of reality. Soon, I no longer trusted anything about myself.

Life moved on, and stepparents were added to the mix. The trauma tub began to fill up quickly, and I felt like I was drowning. Over the next few years, I was passed between two families, with no way to express the emotions that were bouncing around inside me like ping-pong balls. My repressed feelings started to manifest as nervous tics.

It was a blow when my mother uprooted us and took me away from my childhood home and my other family, but I was powerless to stop it. I stuffed my feelings down deep, and tried to adjust. But after my stepfather, in a drunken stupor, announced that Jesus had appeared to him and told him to hang me from a tree and gut me, I knew I needed to get out.

I took the only option available to me at the time: I got married. I was just seventeen.

My boyfriend was the son of a pastor, and had a wonderful, loving family who offered me the safety and support I so desperately needed. I just knew things would be better from then on. My knight in shining armor had rescued me, and I would be safe and happy forevermore.

Within months of our wedding, our honeymoon bliss had already worn off, and my tics began to increase. I realized that I'd gotten myself into bad situation, but I couldn't see a way out. I had made a commitment before God, and it was supposed to be for life.

To fix things, I decided to have a baby. If my husband didn't love me for who I was, I reasoned, a baby would.

Of course, that wasn't the way it went. My tics kept getting worse, and neither my husband nor I knew what was happening to me. He began quoting Scripture at me, to make me "put away childish habits," and "cast away evil things." As the pressure from him intensified, the tics got worse. I felt like a pressure cooker about to explode, but all I knew how to do was internalize, and wonder desperately what I was doing wrong. I felt like there was something I was missing, something I needed to change—but I didn't trust myself to figure out what that something was.

One day, when I was in my early twenties, I turned on the Maury Povich show. His guests were barking and jerking in their seats, and I thought, "Wow! That's me!" I sought out a local neurologist, who confirmed what I had already guessed: I had Tourette's syndrome. He gave me some medication and assured me that I would be okay. I was elated. Finally, I'd be lovable and acceptable again!

Over the next few months, I took my medication faithfully, but while it did suppress the tics, it rendered me completely unable to function. I slept about twenty hours a day. I couldn't take care of my child, and my marriage was unraveling in front of me. My eighteen-month-old, lying on the couch beside me all day, whispering, "Love Mama" and kissing my eyelids, was all I had to keep me from letting go. With my spirit hanging by a thread, I asked myself what I had done to deserve this. How could my fairy tale have turned out this way?

I called my mom to help me, and she moved across the country to do so. Immediately, she weaned me off the medications, and reminded me that I had things to accomplish in this life, tics and all. With her support, I recommitted myself to my children, my marriage, and the world. This time, I decided, life was gonna be good!

By now, my husband had eyes elsewhere, and I needed to do something drastic to get him back. Another child would keep him busy, I thought! The next summer, I gave birth to an amazing little girl, and just *knew* that she would be the glue to hold our family together.

Despite my high hopes, things didn't improve with my husband, and I began to fall into a deep depression. But then, I received a piece of evidence which confirmed that my fears about his wandering weren't just in my head. I decided this was permission for me to trust myself. I wasn't crazy, and I didn't have to take this anymore!

I lost seventy pounds in four months, dyed my hair platinum blond, picked up my babies, and moved out.

All along the way, I'd had a quiet feeling that there was a reason I was experiencing all this. I decided that I wasn't going to stop until I found the answers my heart desired. I'd had a chance to die, and I'd declined to take it. Now I was free, and I had to get back to *me*.

But how?

I truly believe that when you listen to your heart and lead with love, you will end up right where you need to be. That doesn't mean you won't get a little lost along the way. In my quest for answers, not only did I leave my husband with two small children in tow, I also quit my job, ditched the church, screamed at the pastor, slept with the baseball coach, started and folded three businesses, lost a bunch of money, taste-tested several religions, and finally ended up dancing with the wrong man at a restaurant one night, after which his wife burned down their house.

Does it get any better than that? You bet! I started smoking. Menthols.

Still searching for meaning, I decided to really put the pedal to the metal. I delved into meditation, hypnosis, breathing exercises, manifestation, yoga, and everything else I could find on the internet that offered some promise of hope. I wanted to be whole again.

Traumas are only revealed to us at a level at which we can handle them. We have emotional survival mechanisms which protect us until we're ready to heal. When I started meditating, I would often fall asleep, and slip into vivid and revealing dreams. Only now, when I was (barely) able to handle the information, did my dreams show me the sexual trauma I endured as a child—the real reason my mother moved me across the country. I remembered my nightmares, my cravings for real love, and the terror I felt on a daily basis, wondering where my father was and whether he would come home alive. I remembered my grandfather's death, my aunt's suicide, and a hundred other events my mind had buried in order to protect itself.

Slowly but surely, I was able to put together the puzzle of my life, which had previously had so many missing pieces. I had met my shadow, and now it was time to heal.

The healing I experienced over the next few years enabled me to feel joy for the first time in my life, and I knew that if I could find peace after everything I'd been through, others could as well. I wanted to heal the world, and let every woman out there know that she is beautiful, amazing, and powerful. With that goal firmly in mind, I decided to open an integrative medical facility.

It was at this point that I met my current husband and spiritual partner. I recruited him from a local university hospital, and soon found that he had the same passion for integrative medicine that I did. Our joint quest was, and remains, to heal ourselves so completely that we can show others the way to healing. Our journey has taken us over twelve years, and continues to this day.

I truly believe that we must experience that which we wish to teach. If it is not etched in our souls, we cannot have a dramatic impact on others. As hard as it was, I know now that my life path was perfect, because it brought me to a place where I could truly be of service. In the end, it wasn't all about me: it was about the greater good.

Today, I stand before this world whole and holy. I'm the mother of seven beautiful children, the wife of an amazing man, the owner of the Quantum Healing Institute, the director of a Life Transformation course, a poet, a lyricist, a competition dancer, a wellness coach, a naturopath, and more. I'm living a life of abundance, with little to no trace of the Tourette's syndrome I struggled with for so long. I have successfully spoken every emotion from within, and cleared out all those bouncing ping-pong balls.

Will I ever experience conflict and pain again? Of course! They are part of the human experience. But I've learned to accept whatever comes with joy and excitement, because it's part of my transformation. Instead of living in fear, I jump in every day saying, "Bring it on!"

Juicy Questions

Does this story speak to you? The journaling prompts below can help you access messages from your authentic core, and integrate the richness and insights of this story into your own juicy, joyful life!

Do you have a hard time speaking your truth? Do you internalize your emotions, rather than allowing them to be expressed?

_____

_____

_____

_____

How do you think your hidden truths affect your relationship to yourself and the world?

_____

_____

_____

_____

Cynthia believes that we must experience that which we wish to teach. Is there a constructive, creative, or healing way in which you could share your deepest truths with the world?

_____

_____

_____

_____

The End of the Performance

Terri Amos-Britt

I spent a big part of my life believing I had to perform for love. I thought that I had to say the right things, act a certain way, look pretty, and be the best at everything I did. I lived by a belief that said, "You must perform, and do everything right. Then, and only then, will you be loved."

This began to change in 1982 when I won the title of Miss USA. Standing proudly on the stage in that winning moment, my ego said, "Yes!" However, something inside of me felt differently. I heard a voice in my head, asking, "This is it?" Here I was at the peak of my performance—and yet, I felt empty. I thought winning the title of Miss USA would make me feel accepted and loved, like I belonged. But it didn't.

I felt the same way when I started working as an entertainment news anchor in the television industry. Nothing filled me up. None of my successes made me feel loved. That's when I decided, "I don't need this kind of acknowledgment anymore!" I left everything to be a full-time mom.

Boy, was I in for a surprise! Not only did I continue to perform for love, but my performance level escalated to an all-time high! I wanted to be the best mom I could be—and that meant I had to deny myself completely. I truly believed it was my job to make my family happy, and that only by making them happy would I receive their love in return.

What I soon learned was that the more I performed, the angrier I got. Anger was my hidden demon, and had been for years. It burned when the standards I set in my mind weren't met; if I felt that I hadn't done things right, I got mad at myself. But when it really exploded was when someone else didn't do things the way I felt they "should" be done, or when what they'd done didn't fill me up and make me feel happy and loved.

In college, I once slammed my fist into my boyfriend's window. That was a year and a half before I won Miss USA. Can you imagine that? Here I was, a sweet little girl from Arkansas who, in the interview competition, talked about drinkin' beer and dippin' Skoal on the back of a pickup truck—and all the while, there was a monster hiding just beneath the surface, waiting to attack.

My anger didn't stop after I won the competition. I'll never forget the day I slapped my late husband. It was early on in our relationship, and he hadn't acted the way I demanded. Instead of retaliating, he grabbed my hand, laughed at me, and asked, "Is that all you've got?"

It wasn't. My anger reared its ugly head way too often.

I couldn't stand the way I felt, especially when it came to my family. Slowly, I began to realize that not only did I believe I had to perform for love, but I believed my family had to perform, too. I treated my kids the same way I treated myself, believing that I needed to make them "good," so they could seek acceptance and love from the outside world.

My stepson was almost five when I came into his life. He was your typical rambunctious little boy, but back then, I had so many rules about behavior that I often found myself screaming at him. I truly believed that if I made him "be good," he would in turn receive love from others. I remember sitting by his bedside, buried in guilt and remorse, crying, "I don't know how to love you!"

When we had our two little girls it finally hit me: I had to stop the cycle of pain and suffering that had been handed down from generation to generation. If I wanted my family to find peace, love and acceptance, I first had to find those things within myself. That meant I had to stop performing, and be an example for them. I had no idea how this would manifest, but I set an intention to heal.

I started small by taking some classes, hoping that by learning to meditate I could relieve some of my anger and tension. I found myself at an energetic school for healing. My life changed almost immediately. I felt calmer, and yet so alive! Soon, I learned to do healing work with my hands, and decided to dive in to a thirteen-month spiritual counseling class. Woo-hoo! I had finally found my gifts!

Now that I had a spiritual tool chest to help me heal my life, I made a commitment to myself and my family, and took a stand for unconditional love. That meant I had to find the courage to look within, and begin releasing all the rules in my mind. These weren't rules like, "Drive the speed limit." These were ingrained limiting beliefs which told me I must be perfect to receive love. In order to move forward, I had to release all of them, and finally give myself permission to honor, love and accept the way I was created. I had to stop performing!

I was terrified that I would lose my family's love. I knew that in order to honor and love the way I was created, I had to let go of the need to make my family happy. I had to give myself a voice. I had to set boundaries, quit trying to be "good," ask for what I needed instead of just expecting it, stop working so hard, be more playful, give myself permission to be passionate, have an opinion, and feel everything, including anger. In other words, I had to give myself permission to be completely different from how our society says a good mom should be.

But do you know what? I *didn't* lose my family's love. Instead, we got closer. Where our home had been filled with anger, resentment, frustration, and blame, now there was greater communication, joy, acceptance, playfulness, and unconditional love.

My late husband once told me, "I feel better in my skin right now than I've ever felt." When I asked him why, he said, "Because you forced me to it. When you started finding yourself, it forced me to find myself."

I had no idea that by healing my own life, I would give my husband, as well as my family, such wonderful gifts—but I did! Now, those gifts have expanded to touch moms and families all over the world through The Enlightened Mom global community, as I share the tools I've learned for living in unconditional love. By healing myself, I stepped into my life mission.

Today, my life is scrumptiously juicy and joyful. I love being a spiritual coach! And I love being a wife, a mom, and a stepmom. Since my late husband passed, I have remarried, and while I never thought

69

I'd say that I love being a stepmom after the guilt I felt with my late husband's son, I do! My new husband and I have blended our families beautifully by using The Enlightened Mom tools.

Walking this path, I've learned that I don't need to try to control my life or make people love me. Because I have learned to honor and love the way I was created, I can also honor and love the people around me, and receive their love in return. I made the decision to stop performing and, along the way, discovered within myself the unconditional love I'd been searching for.

Juicy Questions

Does this story speak to you? The journaling prompts below can help you access messages from your authentic core, and integrate the richness and insights of this story into your own juicy, joyful life!

Are you performing in some area of your life—at work, for your family, or for your spouse or partner?

_____

_____

_____

_____

Terri once felt that the only way to be loved was to perform. Why do you feel the need to put on an act? What do you hope to achieve?

_____

_____

_____

_____

Living authentically means living from the heart, and from your truth. How is your truth different from the performances you create?

_____

_____

_____

_____

Embracing Peace

Amethyst Wyldfyre

As I approach the half-century mark, my life continues to unfold before me in magical and majestic ways. The journey, while often bumpy, is filled with moments of great joy. But life wasn't always this way for me: the first forty years of my earth walk were filled to overflowing with trauma, self-abuse, and negative thinking.

I am the daughter of an alcoholic father and a codependent mother who suffered from borderline personality disorder. My childhood was one big blur of physical, mental, emotional, and spiritual abuse. My late teens and twenties were spent in a haze of drugs and alcohol, which I perceived as the solution to the pain of growing up in my dysfunctional family. Self-abuse was a way of life for me.

By the time I got married, I'd stopped using cocaine and marijuana, but I was still drinking to the point of passing out, and smoking two packs a day. Then, I found out I was pregnant, and everything came to a screeching halt. I stopped drinking immediately, but I wasn't able to give up smoking for good until I started Lamaze classes. I was going to have a really hard time doing that breathing thing if I was still puffing on a cigarette!

Having my son was one of the most amazing, joyful, miraculous experiences of my entire life—but even this was fraught with drama. I had an emergency C-section, my preemie was in Neonatal Intensive Care, and my husband was so overcome with anxiety and depression that the night we brought our new child home he had a panic attack in the middle of the night. Once the police and the ambulance came to take him away, I was left alone at 3:00 a.m., fresh out of surgery and barely able to walk, to cope with a screaming baby on my own.

By the time my son was six and I was thirty-eight, I realized that my marriage wasn't working anymore. I could no longer take part in maintaining the illusion of "happily ever after," and things were starting to fall apart. Around this time, I took my first yoga class at my gym. I remember it vividly. My life was a chaotic mess. I was working twelve hours or more a day as a real estate developer, caring single-handedly for my son and an anxious, medicated, practically incapacitated husband, and trying to decide whether to brave the dangerous waters of divorce.

The moment I walked into that yoga class, I noticed the teacher immediately. The woman was the perfect embodiment of serenity, grace, presence, and vitality. She practically oozed peace! And for the first time in my life, I was suddenly clear about what I wanted: I wanted that kind of peace. That teacher became my model, my benchmark, an experience of Peace in the flesh.

I had several friends who supported me through the life transition I was making. One asked me a simple question: "What do *you* want?" That question helped me to have the realization that I was actually entitled to want something for myself.

That I could even *have* wants was an entirely new concept for me. I grew up anticipating the needs of others, constantly on the alert for danger, ready to jump in and fix anything that might go wrong. I was the family firefighter. Tension was so normal in my life, and the desire to please such a natural part of my being, that it never occurred to me that I was entitled to contemplate my own needs, or that I deserved to have them fulfilled.

When I finally gave myself permission to explore what I wanted, I learned that Peace was it. No fancy cars, jewelry, or big houses for me—just Peace. This made my work both simple and challenging: wanting a car is pretty simple, but wanting Peace is another story altogether. I created a measuring stick by which to judge all my choices, actions, and experiences. With each act or choice, I asked myself, "Will this bring me closer to Peace? Do I feel more peaceful?" Daily, I asked, "What changes can I make right now which will create more Peace in my life?"

On September 9, 2001, I made my first major move toward Peace: I decided to end my marriage. The day before, we'd celebrated my boy's sixth birthday, and attended my twentieth high school reunion. To make a long story short, my husband's jealous, selfish actions on that day convinced me that our time together was complete. If not for myself, then for my son's emotional safety, I had to make a change.

Two days later, I was heading to court to file the divorce papers when the planes hit the World Trade Center.

Something was in the air that year for all of us. I believe that 2001 marked the start of a massive shift in the collective consciousness which, as of this writing, has yet to culminate. My personal goal for peace began to be echoed by many of the people around me, as both men and women began to wake up to their soul's purpose, and started using their divine gifts to actively create new ways of existing in harmony, joy, creativity, and balance. Healing ourselves, each other, and the planet has become the driving force for multitudes of people—many of whom, like myself, were chosen for a path of service in the healing arts, and to communicate these messages of hope through which we can all dream our new world into being.

Since I made my own inner peace my priority and focus, my life has unfolded like a rose, opening petal by beautiful petal. I have shed my old patterns, fears, and limiting beliefs—sometimes one by one, and sometimes in great chunks—and continue to do so to this day.

When I moved from experiencing moments of Peace two out of thirty days a month to experiencing it twenty-nine out of thirty days, I knew it was time to add another want to my list. This time, I chose Joy.

Now, I realize that the sh*t of my first forty years on this earth has become deep, rich, fertile soil for the sacred garden my life has become. I've planted two seeds, and I'm focused on tending them: Peace and Joy; Joy and Peace.

I am eternally grateful to Spirit for bringing so many beautiful models, teachers, and mirrors into my life, and for providing me with the tools and blessings of health, well-being, creativity, and companionship. I dream that Peace and Joy will make their way into your heart and your life, as they have into mine, and that one day we will awaken to the beauty that life's journey has to offer. Stories of suffering have been told for far too long.

As I continue my own journey, my advice to you is this: remember who you are. You are the light of the world, and Peace is in you. Journey with Joy, and spread the love!

Juicy Questions

Does this story speak to you? The journaling prompts below can help you access messages from your authentic core, and integrate the richness and insights of this story into your own juicy, joyful life!

What do you want more than anything else in the world?

_____

_____

_____

_____

How can you bring this ideal into your life more fully, right now?

_____

_____

_____

_____

Often, we don't know that we desire to embody certain qualities until we see these qualities manifest in other people. Like Amethyst's yoga teacher, these individuals radiate the peace, joy, confidence, or security we want for ourselves. Who in your life is a model for the positive qualities you desire to cultivate? How can you use this person's example as you work to fulfill your own wants and needs?

_____

_____

_____

_____

Happiness is a Decision

Genevieve Kohn

I t was the winter of 1995. I was twenty-three years old and had been in a relationship with Jack (not his real name) for just over two years. I thought I was in love. We'd been living together, and I thought we were headed toward marriage.

Then, he left me.

I'd been struggling with untreated depression since childhood, and had managed to completely center my life around Jack. I hadn't left room for anything other than him in my life, so I thought I had nothing without him. I became suicidal.

Concerned, my mother took me to a psychiatrist for counseling and medication. My stepdad was always there when I needed to share my feelings and fears, as were my dad, stepmom and siblings. I knew that I had many people who loved me, but I was still resentful. I blamed other people—especially Jack and my parents—for the way I felt inside.

After a few months of therapy, I was no longer suicidal, but I was far from healthy. For years, even while I was with Jack, I had been drinking and using other substances, trying to ease my deepening depression. At the time, it was all I knew how to do. I had no tools for living.

That June, I left for grad school in Boston, thinking that a change of location would be the answer to my problems. Of course, this wasn't the case, and what might have been an exciting adventure was actually a very scary time for me. Every day, I tried desperately to escape my feelings—including my growing fear that I had a problem with substance abuse.

I started going to twelve-step meetings, but they didn't help immediately. It wasn't until one morning in March of 1996, after yet another night of "trying" to stop, that I truly realized that the alcohol and substances I was using weren't helping my depression and anxiety: they were actually exacerbating them. If I was ever going to feel better, I needed to stop self-medicating.

Recovery was a slow process, but finally I did stop using alcohol, marijuana and sedatives altogether. I continued going to twelve-step meetings, where I made a few new friends. I also got a steady, good-paying job, and was able to fulfill my dream of vacationing around the country. Inside, however, I was still unhappy. I still blamed other people for the way I felt about myself. I couldn't own up to my part in my own problems. I once blamed a good friend for being upset because I didn't show up for the weekend we'd planned!

At this point, I made the decision to go back into counseling, and take it seriously. I had been in therapy before, after the breakup with Jack, and the antidepressants I was taking did help me function, but I needed something more than that.

Once I participated in it honestly, counseling helped me to see my own patterns of self-sabotage, my desperately low self-esteem, and the ways in which I externalized responsibility. I realized that even though I had hungered within for happiness, I hadn't believed I truly deserved it. To this day I don't know where those feelings came from. However, once I figured out what was going on inside me, I realized that I had choices. No one else was responsible for making me happy. Not Jack, not my parents, not my friends. As an adult, *I was responsible for my own happiness!*

Using the tools I gained through counseling and the twelve-step process, I learned how to take responsibility for my actions and make amends where I had done harm. One by one, I peeled away all those stale layers of behaviors and beliefs, like I was peeling an onion. It wasn't always easy—real growth rarely is—but the work changed my life. I started to realize that happiness isn't a given right: it's something you have to decide to achieve.

By the time I was twenty-nine, I had been living on my own in Boston for six years, and had begun to truly feel happy. I started to notice the gifts in my life, like the love and support my friends and family offered me. I wanted find someone with whom I could share my life and start a family of my own. However, I understood that this might not happen right away, and I had older friends who were single and leading happy, fulfilling lives. I decided that I could be happy either way, single or married, kids or no kids. Plus, I felt I had a little more work to do on myself before I jumped into a relationship.

Then, along came Bill.

He'd started working at my place of employment a few months before. At first, we started talking as friends; then, the relationship deepened. I really didn't think I was ready to fall in love. But it happened anyway.

Since I had learned to love and trust myself, I knew Bill was the right man for me. He was mature and responsible, and he knew what he wanted out of life. He was also seventeen years older than I was.

Six weeks after we started dating, we became engaged, and I had a new set of decisions to make. My mother had passed away due to cancer only a short while before, and I was terrified that I would lose Bill, too. I kept having visions of him having a heart attack or a stroke, or being diagnosed with cancer. I wondered: should I marry Bill, and allow myself to be blissfully happy with him, even if only for a short time? Or should I walk away because of what might happen?

My old fears about not deserving happiness resurfaced with a vengeance, but I couldn't let fear make my choice for me. Instead, I decided to let the facts and my love for Bill guide me. I reminded myself that happiness is a decision, and that I had worked too hard to let this gift slip away.

Nine years of marriage have proven that my fears were unfounded. Bill and I are more deeply in love than ever—and he is still perfectly healthy.

It hasn't always been easy, though. In 2002, I was diagnosed with multiple sclerosis. Again, I had a decision to make: do I let this illness immobilize me, or do I choose health and happiness? When I began to panic, Bill reminded me of our marriage vows: "In sickness and in health." This reminder brought us even closer, and continues to strengthen us today. It also helped us in our decision to start a family despite my diagnosis.

We now have two amazing little boys. They are the most loving people I know. They find joy in everything, and teach me about happiness just by being themselves. In return, I try to teach them to concentrate on the health, happiness, and fun in their lives, rather than the negative things. It is my hope that they will carry their happiness into adulthood, instead of suffering as I did.

My personal experiences have influenced me beyond my family life. Today, I am a certified life/wellness coach and energy healer. My passion is to support others, especially women, and help them realize that they do not have to be held back by depression, anxiety or stress. Like I did, they can *decide* to be happy!

Juicy Questions

Does this story speak to you? The journaling prompts below can help you access messages from your authentic core, and integrate the richness and insights of this story into your own juicy, joyful life!

Do you consistently take responsibility for your own happiness, or do you rely on others to make you happy?

_____

_____

_____

Have you ever had to choose, as Genevieve did, between the path of fear and the path of love? What choice did you make? How do you feel about that choice now?

_____

_____

_____

What is one choice you can make today that will bring you closer to the life you desire?

_____

_____

_____

_____

Worthy of Love

Aimée Yawnick

M y dad moved out before my first birthday. He didn't even come to the party. When I was three the divorce was finalized. My dad signed a piece of paper that said he agreed to give up all rights to me. That's when I made an agreement with myself: I was unworthy of love.

For thirty-five years I kept that agreement, which after a while became a belief, which then became the operating system for my entire life. Whether it was love, money, attention, success, or happiness, if it was something I desired, I believed I couldn't have it because I was not worthy of it.

So, when I finally found my passion and purpose in life coaching and mentoring, it was no big surprise when I struggled to fill my private practice.

Instead of looking inside for the solutions to my challenges, I sought information and advice from outside sources. While I learned a lot about the theory of running a business, none of these sources helped me focus on the one thing that set my business apart from the competition. Nor did they explain that this one thing was so powerful it could sabotage my business at any given moment and stop me dead in my tracks. That one thing, of course, was me!

Although I had the skills to be a great coach and mentor, my ingrained operating system caused me to doubt not only my ability to own and manage a successful business, but my value as a coach and a person. Thanks to my research, I knew everything that I "had to do" to make my business a success, but I still wasn't seeing results, and I felt defeated. Over and over I would ask myself, "What makes you think you can pull this off? Do you really think you're smart enough to run your own business?"

The answer was always the same, "You know you're no good at managing money. That kind of success is for other people, not for you!" It was like there was a broken record playing inside my head.

The power of my limiting beliefs led me to ignore the destructiveness of this negative self-talk. Instead of fighting back and trying to build myself up, I just swept it under the rug, and hoped it would go away. As you can probably guess, that didn't work all that well.

Frustrated, I continued to put all my energy into the assignments I was given by the gurus I was following, but without fail, whenever I would start to see progress, and new clients started coming in, I would find a way to sabotage my efforts, and the phone would stop ringing.

I didn't realize it at the time, but I was locked in a battle between good and evil. You see, I had lost sight of the fact that facing my demons was the only way to disempower them. I was so determined to make my business work that I put myself at the bottom of my to-do list.

Finally, after months on the roller coaster, my already shaky confidence started to plummet. I thought, "I have to figure out a way to make this happen or I'm going to have to close my doors!" My demons chimed in with, "What's wrong with you? Why can't you get this right?" I started to wonder if it was time to consider another 9-to-5 position. If I went back to a regular job, at least the status quo would be maintained, even if there was no chance of making changes—or, heaven forbid, playing a bigger game. In the back of my mind I could hear evil laughter; the demons were rubbing their palms together in vengeful delight.

I told my husband, "I can't do this anymore!"

But even as I threw up my hands in defeat, something magical happened. I started to realize there was a force at play that I had not yet come to fully understand or appreciate. A little voice inside me started to get louder. This voice was not going to let the demons run the show. It told me, "No matter how hard things get, coaching and mentoring women is what you are here to do. You need to suck it up and find a way to create a solution!"

This voice was my Inner Wisdom—my connection to my Self.

In the chaos of information overload, listening to everyone except myself, I lost my connection with my Self. As a coach, I know how crucial this connection is, not only when big events happen, but in everyday life. I realized that to be without it while trying to build my business was professional suicide. In order for me to move forward, I had to do the same hard work I asked of my clients. My old belief system had been causing me to play small for way too long. It was time to stretch beyond my comfort zone, face my fears, step into my purpose, and create something powerful that would serve my greatest desires. It was time to say "Yes!" to my brilliance and allow myself to make the contribution to the world that I knew I was here to make.

The big "Ah-ha!" moment came when was I was working with my own coach. It was one of those moments when you take half a step back to get a different perspective, and everything suddenly comes into focus. Up until then I had believed that I was unworthy of receiving—but it was the belief itself, and not my unworthiness, that kept the things I truly desired out of reach! That belief was the monster of all monsters under my bed. By facing it head on, connecting with my Self, and listening to my Inner Wisdom, I was able to see this clearly for the first time.

It also became profoundly clear that it isn't about *getting*: that is the energy of neediness and not-enoughness. I spent a lifetime trying to get, get, get. I always asked, "What about me?" When I didn't get what I desired, I felt unworthy. But now I understood that the real juiciness is in the value that I have to *give*. Realizing this was like seeing again for the first time after years of blindness—and what I saw was abundance, joy, and pure gratitude.

I have value! I no longer have to fear my gifts, or worry that I am not worthy of my purpose. There is no way that I can have this passion for helping women without having the gift to fulfill that passion!

My entire world changed in that one moment, and I was sure my demons would start an all-out war in retaliation. But they didn't. It was as if they understood the truth of my awareness, and decided I wasn't good prey any longer. I still hear from them every so often, but they no longer frighten me, because I now know that no matter what life sends my way I have a connection with my Self and my Spirit that will guide and support me with grace, love, and confidence. I know that as long as I have breath, I have room for gratitude. I've tapped into my Inner Wisdom, and finally found the success I wanted all along.

Now, it's your turn.

Juicy Questions

Does this story speak to you? The journaling prompts below can help you access messages from your authentic core, and integrate the richness and insights of this story into your own juicy, joyful life!

Do you constantly question your own worthiness? Do you have trouble acknowledging that you deserve good things in your life?

_____

_____

_____

_____

How do your beliefs about yourself hold you back?

_____

_____

_____

Often, our ingrained negative beliefs come out most strongly when we're pursuing something we're passionate about. If you were able to let go of fear and doubt, what passion would you follow? What could you accomplish?

_____

_____

_____

Family MATTERS

Letting Go, Coming Home

RosaLinda Mueller

Thomas Wolfe once said, "You can never go home."

While it's true that we can never go back to the innocence of our childhood, we still carry a trove of treasures and traumas from our past. We never really leave home, because the memories, heartaches, and celebrations are with us wherever we go—in our actions, our hearts, and our very thoughts.

Home is with me, in my feelings and thoughts, memories of the many houses I lived in etched in my mind. Rarely does anyone come into adulthood unscathed by life's challenges, and I am no exception. To really live life, I must relinquish the parts of my past that hold me back, and free myself to live in joy in the present. When I catch myself lost in reverie, I think of how blessed I am to have the home I helped create with my husband of twenty-five years, and feel fortunate to be able to share it whenever I can.

Just recently, I spoke with Mr. Flenory in Kansas City, Missouri. He, his wife, and their two children were thrilled to obtain the keys to their refurbished two-bedroom, two-bathroom house on Chestnut Street. After being evicted from their home through foreclosure, they were now home again! My business partner and I had purchased this house as a bank-owned property, through a program that provides affordable housing opportunities for low- and moderate-income residents. It is very rewarding to me to know that the Flenorys will own their home free and clear in fifteen years, and that their mortgage payment is less than the monthly rent for a similar home down the street.

Speaking to Mr. Flenory brought back memories of my own childhood in a neighborhood called El Sereno, in East Los Angeles.

Like many other barrios, El Sereno was no stranger to drugs, gang violence, teen pregnancies, and other "inner-city" troubles. To reduce our risk of succumbing to these temptations, my parents, on the salaries of a payroll clerk and a Merchant Marine, put all five of us children into parochial schools.

My father was often at sea, and my mother worked long hours. We were often left to our own devices, sometimes in the company of adults who weren't related to us. Yet our mother never made us feel deprived of her time and attention. We were raised on faith and a lot of love.

Growing up, I found freedom and adventure riding my hand-me-down bicycle down the neighborhood streets. My friends and I would ride the four blocks to Johnnie's Market, carrying empty soda bottles to redeem for penny candy. We played softball, flew homemade kites, skinned our knees, bruised our elbows. When the street lights came on, I came home to a kitchen full of the savory aromas of Mexican spices. My mother always cooked for us, even after driving through traffic from downtown Los Angeles after a long day at work.

The neighborhood kids often joined us at the dinner table. It seemed the whole neighborhood felt at home in our little tract house on Thelma Avenue. Later, when my older brother joined the service, he would bring his Navy buddies home with him. Their sleeping bags would line the whole living room. While making them breakfast, I heard their stories of life in Nebraska, Louisiana, even Guam. It didn't bother us to share our single bathroom, and take turns on the few small chairs in the kitchen; it was worth it to see everyone smiling and feeling at home.

My grandmother, calling from her home in Boyle Heights, would say that the house sounded like Grand Central Station. She thought we were always throwing parties she wasn't invited to! Of course, she shouldn't have been surprised: she usually had company in the evenings, too, and would prepare an extra plate for anyone who came to the back door.

When I went away to college, I was fortunate enough to get a position as a nanny to single parents. I became part of these families, and lived in their luxurious homes in the Berkeley hills north of campus. When the mothers traveled, or when their jobs kept them late in the lab or at the office, I tried to bring a sense of security and comfort to the young children under my care. I tried to make home a fun, safe place to be—a place where we made chocolate chip cookies, did homework, and played hide-and-go-seek. When it was time for bed, I chased the eerie sounds out of the darkness, and quieted their cries for Mommy. I promised myself that, when I had small children of my own, I would never leave them for days at a time in the care of a surrogate mother.

Living alone in those big houses while the families were on vacation, I had the opportunity to cook Thanksgiving and Christmas Eve dinners for my college friends, creating a home for us when we couldn't afford to go home for the holidays.

During my college days, I often passed homeless people in the streets on my way to class. I felt so fortunate to have my own room and access to a gourmet kitchen while working my way through college. Although it was sometimes hard to see past their begging hands and urine-stained clothing, I felt connected to them. Before I found the security of my live-in position, I too, was in dire need of money. My desperation led me to sell my plasma on Shattuck Avenue. I knew too well the sting of needles, endured while, on either side of me, an indigent or drug addict made the same agonizing donation.

Also during my college years, my parents divorced. Raising five children—and half the neighborhood—while my father was away at sea took a toll on my mother, and on my parents' relationship. Now that they were separated, there would be no little tract house for me to come home to, no little kitchen to share with my new college friends.

Little did I know that my life was preparing me for greater adventures, and greater responsibility. Instead of going back to El Sereno after college, I landed a job in San Diego. There, I met my future husband, a divorced father of four sons. I dove headfirst into matrimony and motherhood. With my naïveté and optimism, I thought I could I could move into the old family house, and commence providing my new family with a secure, loving, happy home—the kind of home I'd always wanted for myself.

It wasn't quite that easy. The boys had already been through so much stress and uncertainty—and now, they had to try to accept me as the woman of the house, a position their birth mother had resigned. I never realized how much pain and sadness they would feel, missing their mother's presence in the familiar rooms of their house. It was a lot to handle, but with time, patience, prayer, and many tears, the love I had for them and their father, and the love they had for each other, was enough to make our family work. Home became a place of acceptance, where we felt free to just *be*; a safe place where we could laugh, cry, or even scream, and no one would judge or question.

Throughout the years we were blessed with three more children. During that time, we often opened our home to others. Whether our guest was a friend who needed a place to stay while completing a medical residency, or a friend going through a divorce, we always had an extra room. At one time, we opened our home to someone living on the streets. A hot shower and a warm bed seemed a small price to pay for the immense joy and gratitude expressed by our new friend.

All of my experiences have prepared me to fulfill a bigger purpose in life that I never dreamed possible. I have experienced the pain of losing a family home, the grief of losing babies to miscarriage, and the triumph of graduating college. I've been blessed to marry the man of my dreams, and raise our seven children. And I have learned to move beyond my circumstances, beyond my triumphs and tragedies, to forgive the people in my life who should have been there for me—who should have offered me protection and guidance, when I was left unsupervised as a child to be harmed by other adults—but who were themselves too broken or hurt to do so. Through faith, I found a home within myself, a place where I was at home in my own skin. And so I was given the privilege of transforming what could have been an unsettled and conflicted home into a place of unconditional love and acceptance.

I thank God every day that I have the ability to open my heart and my doors to those in need. I've learned that when I give my time and attention to people, I am able to transform my relationships with them into ones of trust, love, and pure joy; then, they can in turn open their hearts to others.

Now, our last three children have gone away to college, but the deafening sounds of "Grand Central Station" still echo in the house. We still hear the sounds of loud music, and step over wall-to-wall comforters and pillows in the family room floor when our children come home to visit. I look forward to the laughter and chaos of our crazy, cozy, joy-filled home. My children know that they can *always* come home, and that home is with them wherever they go.

Juicy Questions

Does this story speak to you? The journaling prompts below can help you access messages from your authentic core, and integrate the richness and insights of this story into your own juicy, joyful life!

Where do you feel most at home? What characteristics of this place define "home" for you?

_____

_____

_____

_____

How can you share the joys of your home with others?

_____

_____

_____

What features of your childhood home define you? Do you feel that they hold you back? What can you let go of in order to create a more positive space for yourself and your family in the present moment?

_____

_____

_____

_____

In the Eyes of a Child

Dianne C. Nassr

As the doctors handed me my newborn girl for the first time, our eyes met, and my heart suddenly overflowed with a love I had never before experienced. Here in my arms was the miracle of life. Suddenly, I realized that I was a mother, and Rena was my daughter!

I thanked God for this gift of a healthy child, and realized how strong my faith had become since I became pregnant. Who but God could create such a perfect miracle? I was confident that I was going to be a good mom, and looked forward to watching Rena grow and achieve her dreams.

I was fortunate enough to spend all of Rena's childhood at home with her and her two siblings. The years passed quickly. Before I knew it, Rena had fallen in love. She had a beautiful storybook wedding, and her life seemed to be moving in an exciting direction.

One Thanksgiving, Rena and her husband arrived at our house with joyful expressions on their faces. "I'm pregnant!" Rena exclaimed. My husband and I were thrilled to hear that our first grandchild was on the way!

Rena was scheduled for her first doctor's appointment the following week. During the exam, the doctor had difficulty visualizing the embryo by ultrasound. Anxiety and confusion consumed everyone's hearts and minds. Unfortunately, soon after that exam, Rena's pregnancy ended in a devastating miscarriage.

When I heard the news, my whole body went numb, and a feeling of helplessness came over me. The doctors had no explanation for what had happened. We could only assume that God had other plans for Rena. We prayed for our daughter and her husband, hoping they would have the courage to try to conceive again in the future.

The miscarriage was a tragedy in Rena's life, but we all felt her pain. Our family bonded together during this time, in a way that we'd never needed to do until then.

Having placed more than eighty infants for adoption over the course of my former career as a social worker, I began to wonder if God had given me that experience so I could prepare my daughter to adopt a child of her own. Each infant I worked with became very special to me, and I felt confident that any child would benefit from Rena's loving home. Was this God's plan for our family? Only time would tell.

During another visit several months later, Rena told us that she was pregnant again. Cheers of joy filled the house as we celebrated this new promise of a family for my daughter and her husband. Rena's doctor had assured her that this time she was going to be fine, and that she should not worry; she was very healthy, and he fully expected an easy pregnancy.

After reaching the three month mark without any sign of trouble, Rena said, "Let's tell the rest of the extended family." We couldn't wait to share the good news with our relatives around the country.

Two days later the phone rang. My husband answered. Suddenly, tears began to fall from his eyes.

"Who is it?" I asked. "What's happening?"

"It's Rena," he answered. "We need to get to the hospital. She's having another miscarriage!"

Tears flowed as we drove to the hospital, which was fifty miles away. We arrived just in time for me to look into Rena's eyes, and see the heartache she was feeling, before she was whisked away for surgery.

That night, we drove Rena home, and tried to make sense of what had just happened. "But the doctor said everything was fine," she kept saying to me. "Mom, I'm healthy. There's nothing wrong with me. How could this happen a second time?"

I wished I knew the right thing to say to my daughter, but I didn't: no words could describe how we were feeling at that moment. I could only remind Rena of our faith, and hope that faith would comfort her.

"God has a plan for each of us," I told her, "We just need to trust in His plan."

Rena's second miscarriage shifted our whole family dynamic. Not only was our bond of love strengthened even more, but Rena began to see me in a new role. She began to allow herself to receive my love on a level that she could not prior to this tragedy. Was that God's intent?

Two short months later, during a Sunday family dinner, my daughter quietly announced that she was pregnant for a third time. We were overjoyed, of course, but we expressed it cautiously, because we knew we had a long road ahead, with both physical and emotional challenges to overcome.

An ultrasound was scheduled for the following Tuesday. I sat by the phone, waiting for Rena's call. At 9:30 a.m. the phone rang. Although I was shaking with nervousness, I kept my voice calm. "Hi honey. How did it go?" I asked.

Rena was very emotional, and couldn't speak for a moment. "Mom," she finally gasped. "I'm having twins! God brought them both back to me!"

Now, I knew her tears were happy ones. I said the first words that came into my mind. "Yes, of course! One didn't want to come without the other!" We both laughed in shock and relief at the news. More tests revealed that the twins were going to be identical. What a wonderful double blessing!

The next seven months were painfully long. As each milestone was reached, we celebrated and expressed gratitude to God for the beautiful boys growing inside Rena. Due to the doctor's availability and the need to schedule an operating room, the date of April 1st was chosen for Rena's Caesarian section. It was not an April Fool's joke, though initially we questioned the choice of date with a chuckle.

The birth went perfectly. Both children emerged into the world healthy and strong. My husband and I were able to hold these miracles of life in our arms just moments after their births. I looked into my grandsons' eyes, and discovered a whole new type of love in my heart.

As I watched Rena hold her newborns for the first time, I remembered how special that moment had been for me, more than thirty years before. At that moment, her heartache was healed, and the room was overflowing with love. The circle of life was now complete.

During a visit to Rena's house three days later, I laid the babies on the bed next to each other. They naturally turned to face one other. Then, I noticed that Michael had reached over to take his brother Luke's hand. The sight of these newborn babies looking at each other with such love and affection will forever stay imprinted in my heart. Truly, God understood that neither wished to enter this world without his brother.

My miracle grandchildren radiate love and happiness upon every member of our family, and it gives us great joy to watch them grow. The loving bond between twins cannot be described in words, simply observed and cherished as God's gift to us all.

Juicy Questions

Does this story speak to you? The journaling prompts below can help you access messages from your authentic core, and integrate the richness and insights of this story into your own juicy, joyful life!

Has there been a situation in your life where a tragedy has been revealed as a blessing?

_____

_____

_____

_____

How can a shift in perspective help you focus on the positive—in any situation?

_____

_____

_____

_____

Family, whether inherited or chosen, is very important to us all. How has your own family (or family of friends) helped you to stay positive during difficult times? How have you done the same for them?

_____

_____

_____

_____

Blessings in Disguise

Amy Thoreson

"It's a girl!" I hear, as the doctor hands my precious premature daughter to one of four neonatal nurses hovering nearby. I barely get a glimpse of her small, frail body through all the nurses and doctors crowded around me and the two incubators. My thirteen-and-one-half-week-early babies will be cradled by sterile clear plastic boxes, instead of in my loving arms.

"Jim, I can hardly see her," I sob, hearing her meek cry.

"That's good," the doctor says, "Her lungs are stronger than we thought they'd be. Most babies born at twenty-six weeks don't even make a sound."

It's a small reassurance. "She's so little, she's so little," I continue to repeat, still trying to see her through the bodies of those who huddle around her, trying to save her life.

"Amy, focus! You have another one about to be born." The delivery OB brings me back to reality. There's still another life inside me, all too eager to come in to this world.

With the next contraction, our second child makes her presence known with her own stronger cry. She is younger—but at one pound, fourteen ounces, she weighs eight ounces more than her sister. She is whisked into another stranger's arms and wrapped in sterile garments to await the same multitude of tests. The nurses and doctors huddle over her, hooking up IVs, attaching tubes and wires to monitor her every movement and breath. The neonatal doctor feels our second child is stable enough to be briefly held up for me, her mommy, to see, although she is still fifteen feet away. Then, in what seems like an instant and an eternity at the same time, she's whirled away in her incubator to join her sister in the Neonatal Intensive Care Unit. I wonder: will they make it long enough for me to see them again?

For almost two months, we experienced a constant yo-yo of emotions. Bridget, the younger of the twins, improved steadily, getting bigger and stronger every day. On the other hand, Amber, our firstborn, had us on enough of a roller coaster ride for the two of them combined. Amber made some great strides, like breathing on her own for six days at just over two weeks old—but then she had tummy issues and was put on antibiotics a few times, and also needed surgery. Despite the setbacks, each good day gave us great hope.

Eventually, though, her kidneys started to shut down from all the stress. After fifty-five days of complete joy and devastating fear, Amber left us.

Even when I was very young, I'd dreamed of having twin girls. When I found out we were expecting twins, I was above Cloud Nine. When they were born prematurely, I still remained positive that my dream was coming true. But when we lost Amber, I lost myself and my dream. I lost all sense of ever dreaming or hoping again. Amber was gone, and I was gone, too.

Bridget came home from the hospital one month after Amber died. Trying to take care of a preemie, my husband, and my empty self was difficult at best. I spent the next two years feeling lost and resentful—not at anyone in particular, but at life. In my eyes, God had let me down. Jim and I grew further and further apart. The only thing that kept me going was Bridget: she needed me, and I needed her.

I don't remember when I finally realized I couldn't continue being angry anymore. I think it was something I knew all along, but had refused to see. In retrospect, my anger was my way of letting God down. Finally I just said, "Enough, Amy, move on!"

Five years prior to my pregnancy, Jim and I were introduced to some great motivational and self-improvement books. When I decided it was finally time to get on with life, I picked up a couple of those books and started re-reading them. I started working on myself physically and emotionally. Jim and I sought counseling, and started communicating and working on our relationship again. We didn't want to separate, although during those first two years after Bridget came home, the D-word was thrown around a lot; now, I know this was due to the fact that both of us were grieving differently. We decided that we didn't want to become a statistic, and we didn't want Bridget being brought up in a broken home. We were determined. Just as a friendship needs both parties to be involved, or else the relationship withers and dies, a marriage takes commitment and work to succeed. Both parties have to dance the dance, and walk the walk, together.

Jim and I slowly grew closer again, regaining the love, respect, and patience we'd once had for each other. Life seemed to be going smoothly.

Then, when Bridget was six and a half, our son was born via a very scary emergency C-section. Eighteen months later, we had an unexpected pregnancy. Our newest daughter became severely ill with food allergies at fourteen months old, and was sick for several months. Six months after that, I was diagnosed with thyroid cancer. My life was a back-to-back progression of turmoil and fear.

I hungered for a way to heal my family and myself. I knew life wasn't meant to be like this. Information regarding creative visualization, meditation, and natural healing began to flow to me as I looked for ways to help our youngest daughter, and then myself.

A few years later, I heard about the Law of Attraction. I didn't understand before how when I'd chosen to be angry or bitter, it affected *all* aspects of my life—not just today, but long term. Conversely, when I choose to be happy and grateful, it brings about more good things.

Today, I am much more positive. I know our family has gone through what we have for a reason. I even know what some of those reasons are, and I've realized that other people can benefit from what we've gone through, and what we've learned. Someone I deeply respect said recently, "Nothing is wasted by God. He'll always draw good out of suffering. It's our choice to trust in Him." I think deep down, I knew this all along, but sometimes when things come to us at certain points in our lives, we just aren't ready to hear or accept them.

There's a bigger picture than just ours. Each of us has a part to play in life. When we make the best of each situation that arises, that's when magic happens. We become an inspiration to others, and the ripple effect begins.

I am grateful for the path I've been on, and I don't dwell on the fact that I've lost a child, or survived cancer. Of course, it's still painful to think of Amber—especially when we celebrate Bridget's birthdays and other life events—but whenever I help someone see they can choose to *create* their life by choosing how they react to it, or explore natural prevention and healing, I'm at peace, knowing that Amber's life, and death, had a purpose. I hope that my story will help you grow to understand that even the worst tragedies can be blessings in disguise, if we choose to view them from a place of faith and love.

Juicy Questions

Does this story speak to you? The journaling prompts below can help you access messages from your authentic core, and integrate the richness and insights of this story into your own juicy, joyful life!

Has there been a tragedy or setback in your life that you feel holds you back?

_____

_____

_____

_____

If you could change the influence this past event or situation holds over your life today, how would your life change for the better?

_____

_____

_____

_____

What positive lessons can you take from your past experiences? How can you share these lessons with others to inspire positive growth?

_____

_____

_____

_____

Burning the Candle

Amy O'Connor

"Don't burn the candle at both ends!"

My mother frequently used that expression during my first year of marriage, sixteen years ago. I never gave it too much thought—until one cold December, when my perfect world came crashing down, and harsh reality finally set in.

Until that point, I'd thought my life as The Doctor's Wife was just peachy. What more could I want? I was blessed with a loving, supportive family, strong friendships, and a caring husband with whom I'd had three adorable children in four years. Our weeks were full of activities and sports; our weekends were full of parties. So what was missing? Why was I walking on eggshells in my own home?

The abilities to gloss over confrontational issues and deny uncomfortable truths were attributes I thought every good wife should have. I liked to keep the peace in our home, and would make every attempt not to "trigger" my husband. The problem was, I could never figure out what might set him off.

From the beginning of our marriage, I saw our family life break down into two parts: my husband, busy building a successful practice, and me and the kids showing him that we were thriving. I wanted my husband to be proud of me. I wanted him to tell his mother what a good sport I was because I never complained about how many hours he worked. I wanted him to boast that I was Super-Mom. Since I am an approval-seeker, all of this made perfect sense to me. I felt it was my job to regulate our home environment, control our hectic lifestyle, and have a hot meal on the table when my husband came home. He couldn't find fault with me if I had all this all under control, could he?

Unfortunately, it was never good enough.

A palpable nervous tension filled our house. No one knew what the repercussions would be if my husband had a bad day at work. His obsessive-compulsive behaviors were getting worse. He would always blow the driveway clear of all debris before coming into the house. Fingerprints on the glass door were the bane of his existence. Predicting what would cause a blowup in our home was impossible.

And so I walked on eggshells, over-accommodating to protect the kids and myself from confrontation. I manipulated situations to look more favorable than they were, and became more passive-aggressive every day. As my husband's controlling ways became more pronounced, I fell into his web of domination. My stubbornness prevented me from admitting what I was feeling. Facing my reality was to be avoided at all costs. A marriage that didn't go according to plan simply wasn't part of my value system.

Or was it?

My mom's axiom kept ringing in my ears—but keeping busy with my kids and personal activities meant I did not have to face my own reality. Deep down, I knew that I had a great life, but a horribly contemptuous marriage. Instead of addressing the resentment growing between us, I tuned my husband out as often as possible, and continued making excuses for poor behavior on both our parts. When we scheduled a family portrait with a professional photographer and my husband forgot to show up, I swept it under the rug. The excuses came naturally to me. He was working so hard to build his practice: who was I to complain?

All the while, my walls were getting higher and more difficult to breach. I felt justified in giving him the cold shoulder and withholding my true feelings, thinking that this would be punishment enough to force him to change. By enabling his dysfunction and not standing up for what I knew was right, I allowed his personality to get bigger, while I kept shrinking.

All of our charades came at a price. The person who meant the most to me was slowly slipping away, and our life was spiraling out of control.

The tidal wave finally hit in December. I was dealing with holiday stresses, going full-tilt to a zillion parties, and living with unrelenting dysfunction. But it was the fact that my children were starting to model my husband's disrespectful behavior towards me that finally made me snap. I had reached my breaking point. My wall, once as strong as Berlin's, came crashing down. It was time to grow up and face reality. I could not go on with my marriage the way it was.

We cried together for days for what our marriage had become. Our mutual disrespect, lack of communication, resentment, and years of passing blame took over, and won. But even through this, a little voice in the back of my head kept saying, "You owe it to yourself and your kids to try and save this marriage. You have never been a quitter."

After hours of talking, we concurred that the excuses we had made for our marriage were no longer acceptable, and that we needed marriage counseling immediately. We couldn't go on with life as we knew it, so we had to take on the challenge of changing our ways.

A fabulous couples' therapist in Boston was recommended to us, and we had an appointment within a week. He turned out to be our lifeline. A few short months and a lot of hard work later, we were on the road to recovery. Our therapist's direct approach empowered us, and diving into various workshops allowed us to open our hearts to each other and be vulnerable in ways we didn't know were possible. After sixteen years, we finally exposed our true selves to each other.

113

God works in mysterious ways, and I feel like there is a reason we hit rock bottom. It took years of pent up frustration, many blowouts, and deep resentments to make us surrender to one another. The love was there all along, but was overshadowed by immaturity, and the fact that neither of us knew how to have a healthy relationship. I would not be the person I am today if we hadn't figured out our dysfunctional dance, and worked to correct it.

Living a truly respectful life means you can't rationalize. You can't say that your marriage "isn't that bad." I knew of many relationships that were worse than mine; why should I deserve better? I thought that because I wasn't being physically abused, a marriage counselor seemed unjustified. Asking someone to listen to my disheartened tales of fighting and sadness seemed futile. I was convinced that self-help books could help us get through our "rough patch."

What I didn't realize was that, by denying my reality, I was only harming myself.

After my personal experience with a marriage on the brink of disaster, I became acutely aware of a passion to help couples and individuals find health and serenity in both marriage and life. With my husband's encouragement, I pursued my dream, and trained in the same model of marriage and life therapy which worked so effectively for us. My gift is to help those in need of guidance, just as we were helped.

Burning the candle at both ends implies that the candle will burn out twice as fast as a candle with one end burning alone. It's also a warning that the person doing the burning will eventually be the one who is burned. Putting on a happy face when you're not really happy is a major disservice to yourself, and to those you love.

I have realized that you can't change anyone else; you can only change yourself. The more I accept this truth, the more empowered I become. I will forever hold my feet to the fire, and make myself responsible for my actions and feelings. No more excuses.

The tools to create a healthy marriage and family life were inside me all along. Since we started holding ourselves accountable, and stopped playing the toxic blame game, my husband and I have never been happier. My outlook on life has changed dramatically, as has my appreciation, compassion, and respect for my marriage and my family. We will never turn back to our old ways again.

Juicy Questions

Does this story speak to you? The journaling prompts below can help you access messages from your authentic core, and integrate the richness and insights of this story into your own juicy, joyful life!

Often, when we think we're hurting or punishing others with our behavior, we're only hurting ourselves. Where in your life have you experienced this?

_____

_____

_____

Marriages, like all relationships, are partnerships, and there is a definite need for give-and-take. What does an equal partnership look like to you? Do you find yourself assuming a dominant role, or a subservient role as Amy did? If so, what steps can you take to regain equal footing with your partner?

_____

_____

_____

When their marriage looked like it was about to fall apart, Amy and her husband decided to stick it out. Looking back on your own life, are there situations where you're glad you stuck it out, no matter how hard it was at the time? What did you learn from these experiences?

_____

_____

_____

Breaking the Cycle

Heidi Reagan

L ong before handheld video games and in-car DVD players were the rage, most children would moan and groan on long trips, asking "Are we there yet?" Not me, though. I was thrilled to ride shotgun in our 1960 Volkswagon Beetle, cruising down the highway with my mom behind the wheel. This was our special time, and during every trip, without fail, we would sing the songs she had taught me during previous road trips. It wasn't often that we would jump in the Bug to visit family or friends—but when we did, oh what a time it was. Belting out show tunes, ballads, and '60s pop songs, we were just two carefree girls on the open road.

Those were the memories I clung to when I arrived home after school and let myself into our apartment to wait alone until Mom got home from work. We'd been on our own from the time I was an infant, and although peace, love, and rock'n'roll were the themes of the '60s, our neighborhood was still in the *Leave It to Beaver* era, and I was very aware of the differences between our family unit and others in our town. Still, I took pride in Mom. She was so stylish, with her tailored coats, monochromatic color combinations and pill box hats; a real fashion maven. She had a much more interesting history than other moms, too: at one time or another, she'd been a magazine model, a roller derby girl, and a blue grass singer on tour with the then-famous Earl Scruggs.

Yes, I had a cool mom—a strong, independent thinker, a warrior of sorts. She took her job as a mother seriously, and was always working to improve our living situation. That meant that we moved every year from 1965 to 1972. Mom worked hard, and never stopped searching for that new job which would bring us closer to the security I later realized she was so desperately seeking.

Each move brought me to a new school, where I needed to make new friends. Working to break into the social scene of a group of kids who had often been together since kindergarten was frightening and painful. It was almost easier to keep to myself, avoid the rejection, and wait for the transition that inevitably came. It wasn't until I was in my twenties that I realized I wasn't an introvert at all. I actually enjoyed meeting new people; it was the experience of rejection which taught me to stifle my natural tendency to socialize.

The vulnerability, loneliness, and fear which consumed my mother became more apparent with each new job and change in location. As I became privy to that side of her personality, I decided that it wouldn't be fair to share the emotional turmoil I was in. It was my job, I decided at the tender age of eight, to disconnect from my needs in order to make life easier for Mom, and spare her any further uneasiness. It was a belief I lived for many years.

As I moved into adulthood, one thought was prevalent: when I married, it would be forever, and my children would have the stability I didn't. Boy was I shocked when, after eighteen years of marriage and with an eight-year-old daughter, I discovered that I had in fact recreated the very pattern from my own childhood I'd struggled to leave behind. Sure, my marriage lasted longer than my parents' had, but somehow I'd managed to find myself alone with my only daughter when she was just eighteen months old, after my husband took a government job on an island in the South Pacific where no family members were allowed to live. He would return home briefly every eight weeks, but I was still essentially a single mom. How had I allowed this to happen? How had I allowed the one pattern I was determined to prevent, to prevail?

In an effort to make my then-husband happy during his visits home, we had moved three times. The last move took us to an isolated 120-acre homestead in the Ozark Mountains. My husband was a country boy by nature, and spending ten months a year on a two-mile-long piece of coral in the South Pacific was taking its toll on him. To him, coming home to wide-open spaces, trees, and grass, through which he could roam at will, was his saving grace. But, in the course of making his dream a reality, I—a suburban New Jersey gal—found myself alone in the middle of nowhere, with one darling little girl named Carly, one black lab, and one Ford F-150 pickup truck. What was I thinking?

Once, I'd worried about my mother's fragile state; now, my concern was keeping my husband happy and stress-free when he came home from the island. That would have been fine with me, had it also been the best situation for my daughter and I, but neither of us thrived in isolation. After three years of waking up at 2:00 a.m. and stumbling outside in twenty-degree weather to add wood to our outdoor furnace—our only heat source—I realized I was perpetuating a pattern I did not want to pass on to my only daughter. The suburbs I'd grown up in were certainly different from the hills of Missouri, but I had often sensed that my mother resented having no one to fall back on when challenges came up for her. Now, I was becoming resentful, and Carly was picking up on it. It was time to break the cycle.

I was suddenly aware that I no longer needed to chop up the poisonous copperheads that crawled through our kitchen because it was too dangerous to catch them. I didn't need to struggle to change another flat tire on the roadside just because my husband loved our two-mile gravel driveway. It was time to tap into my personal strength and make one final move.

We headed back to more familiar territory, New York State. The dream of living happily ever after had disintegrated long before, but that move was what really ended my marriage. It was clear that my husband and I were very different people with different goals and desires, and that staying married for Carly's sake alone was not a healthy solution. We split, and though her father remained an active part of her life, Carly and I picked up where we left off: just the two of us, going it alone.

After moving to New York, I was determined to create a different school experience for Carly than I had endured. When she was in second grade, I enrolled her in the local elementary school, and she remained there until she graduated from eighth grade. I saw what a difference that stability made for her, as she developed strong friendships and grew more secure within herself every year.

As she grew older, I found that Carly worked to take care of my feelings, as I had tried to take care of my mom's. But we learned how to communicate with one another about our challenges, frustrations and triumphs, and honor our individual needs and feelings. We discovered how to overcome obstacles without turning to guilt, fear, or anxiety. When I start to take things too seriously, no one can make me laugh like Carly, with her unique sense of humor and storytelling abilities.

In one year, my daughter heads off to college, and I will officially be an "empty nester." For a single mom and an only child, that separation can hold a different meaning—especially when mom and daughter are as close as Carly and I. However, I am confident that we will both approach this new experience with a sense of fearlessness and appreciation, because we have learned to stand strong in our individual truths. We have broken the cycle.

Juicy Questions

Does this story speak to you? The journaling prompts below can help you access messages from your authentic core, and integrate the richness and insights of this story into your own juicy, joyful life!

We all learn patterns—emotional, physical, and spiritual—from our parents and role models. What patterns in your life were passed down from previous generations?

_____

_____

_____

_____

What cycles in your life do you believe are important to pass on to your children? Which cycles do you think it's important to break?

_____

_____

_____

_____

If you have a cycle you'd like to stop, break down your behavior pattern into three sections: trigger, reaction, and consequence. Heidi's cycle was triggered by her husband's needs, and her reaction was to place his happiness before her own. The consequence was a long struggle for both her and her daughter. What triggers your own cycles? How can you change your reaction to create a new consequence?

_____

_____

_____

Fear
IS NOT A FACTOR

Access Your Power

Laurie McAnaugh

It's important to me that I choose, every day, to be a person who makes a difference in the world. For several years, my daily mantra has been, "Show me the way to serve for the greatest good of all." But for a long time, my very next thought was, "What could I possibly have to offer anyone?"

I've been inspired by many books and personal lectures from "the greats." All of them seem to have a story. Some grew up in orphanages; others battled grave illness or poverty, or were abused as children. Me? I grew up with two parents who are still madly in love with each other, their children, and even both of their sons-in-law. I have an amazing and supportive husband who has adored me since I was sixteen years old. There was no abuse, no tragic event; no *story*. I couldn't help but wonder: who would ever listen to me?

Little did I know, I *did* have a story. I just hadn't uncovered it yet.

Despite my "easy" life surrounded by love, I grew up afraid. From my earliest childhood until the age of thirty-two, I lived every single day worrying that I would die. And I don't just mean I worried a little: I obsessed over dying so much that at various times in my life, I allowed my obsession to consume me.

While I was growing up, I became focused on the challenges other teens faced. This left me with the constant hovering thought, "When will my personal 'bomb' drop? When will it all fall out from under me?" It was a private battle, hidden from my family and the outside world: in fact, I had no real awareness that I lived that way, or that my fear held me back at all.

As I got older, the anxiety I felt began to take a physical toll. My hormone levels were all over the place. At one point, my doctor prescribed a short cycle of a synthetic hormone.

A few weeks after completing the medication, my story really began to unravel before me. My daily "normal" fears started to intensify, gradually leading to loss of appetite and a growing disinterest in leaving the house.

The lowest point is a moment I will never forget. The picture I'd held of myself up until then was of a confident, independent woman. That image was shattered that day, as my fear truly became the victor. I attached myself to my husband's leg, begging him to stay home from work to keep me safe. He was heartbroken, and as he dragged me across the kitchen floor, he screamed through tears of helplessness, "What are you afraid of?"

My only reply was, "I don't know." I had no explanation for the sheer terror that permeated every cell of my body. Here I was, surrounded by love in my beautiful home, with my healthy and incredible children, living my charmed life—and yet I was filled with fear.

What I *did* know was that I needed help. I also knew I was ticked off. I was angry that the strong, incredible, talented and confident woman I knew was inside me refused to show her face.

Medication was not an option for me (after all, what if I died of an allergic reaction?) so I forced myself to find alternative ways of healing. Through divine intervention, I came across a series of tapes on anxiety and depression which literally changed my life.

I still remember the day the box came in the mail. I was so skeptical: how could I possibly be suffering from *that*? I was still convinced that the only thing that was wrong with me was that I was going to die, and I had a whole list of symptoms and ailments to prove it!

With my husband's prodding, I opened the box and with each description I read, hope began to wash over me.

Each tape opened with a statement like, "I know you're thinking you can skip this lesson because *you* don't suffer from *this*, but I will tell you, listen anyway!" So whether the tape covered panic attacks or self limiting beliefs, I convinced myself to listen even though I "knew" I had no use for that session. Of course, each and every one of those twelve tapes described how I had lived my entire life.

From that moment on, I became a student of growth and development. Slowly, the cast of voices inside my head began to change their lines. I learned to release my fear of dying, and began to take responsibility for not only how I'd chosen to live up until that point, but who I wanted to become, and how I wanted to show up in the world moving forward. I delved into lessons from those who have paved the way for self discovery, people like Wayne Dyer, Carolyn Myss, and Eckhart Tolle. I began to cultivate an awareness of my own thought patterns and belief systems—thoughts I'd had no idea I held, beliefs which had never served me or anyone in my presence. Those damaging patterns, I learned, went way beyond my fear of death.

Through my painful journey, I gained the wisdom I needed to be able to help others as I'd always wanted to do. I am grateful to have the opportunity to share what I have learned along the way. The power we need to release the grip of fear and be happy, successful, and fulfilled already exists within us. It can't ever leave us, because we were born with it. The core of who we are is already amazing, and needs no improvement. An understanding of that concept gives us the tools to access that power. Make no mistake about it: accessing your power is a choice.

For a long time, I yearned to live my life as the powerful, confident woman I knew was inside of me. What I learned was that being powerful was less about standing up to others, and more about standing up to that voice inside my own head that was always whispering, "I'm not enough" and "What if I fail?"

Accessing your power means choosing to listen to only one internal voice—the one that says, "This is the skin I'm in, and I'm good with that, no matter what."

Today, I am humbled and honored to work with people from around the country who feel what I once felt, and help them to discover their own value. To me, being powerful means being confident, showing compassion to yourself and others, and living in a constant state of gratitude and optimism. It means taking nothing personally, and seeking to surround yourself with those who inspire you towards greatness, while consciously avoiding the drama and chaos that drags you down. Most importantly, it means accepting forgiveness as your *only* option, while willingly assuming 100% responsibility for your thoughts, actions, successes, and failures.

Now, eight years after that terrible day in the kitchen, I know that my sense of self-worth is the single most important quality I can choose to build and strengthen. Today, I am grateful. I am compassionate.

I am powerful.

Juicy Questions

Does this story speak to you? The journaling prompts below can help you access messages from your authentic core, and integrate the richness and insights of this story into your own juicy, joyful life!

Is there a specific point in your life when you decided to access your power? How did you do this?

_____

_____

_____

_____

Do you live with unspoken fears? How do these fears keep you from living a full, juicy life?

_____

_____

_____

_____

What is one step you can take toward conquering your deepest fear?

_____

_____

_____

_____

From Fear to Liberation

Dianna Sandora

"Delight thyself also in the LORD; and He shall give thee the desires of thine heart." – *Psalm 37:4*

I f you knew me, you might not believe this story. But then, most people who thought they knew me did not. I have always tried to be optimistic, smiling, quick to laugh. For a long time, though, on the inside, I was in a constant state of fear.

I spent my life trying to be what I thought everyone else wanted. I strove to be the perfect daughter, the perfect student, the perfect friend, the perfect wife. I always had negative voices in my head—and what is worse, I listened to them. While I lived a blessed life, my life was far from what it could have been, because I lived with this unexplainable fear of rejection and failure.

Ironically, most people I met loved me immediately, and most things I attempted to do were not failures. Still, I was not able to find any real peace or satisfaction. For a while, I tried to find comfort in simply existing: if I did not focus on what I was going to be when I grew up, I did not have to worry about the voices telling me that I would never be good enough to be whatever I tried to become.

My fears made happiness in my marriage very difficult as well, because I was not really being myself. If I was drawn away from my focus on my husband, Tony, and started concentrating on something I wanted, I would begin to feel guilty and uncomfortable. Our relationship became symbiotic; I began to feel that my very existence depended on him. Instead of changing my behavior, I decided that this was the way it was. While my life might not be perfect, I had more than most.

When all the financial trouble happened in 2008, Tony lost his job. When he couldn't find work after a year, the decision was made that he should go back to school. He had always wanted to work on motorcycles, so we found the best school available. The only challenge: it was three hours away. Since traveling back and forth every day did not make sense, he stayed with friends during the week. We would talk on the phone and send text messages, and he would come home on the weekends.

I did not realize it then, but this was the best thing that could ever have happened to me. For the first time in a long time—if ever—I had the opportunity to get to know myself. Prior to this, every decision I'd made was about what Tony wanted. After he left for school, I had to learn how to be by myself. I had to make simple decisions about what to watch on television, or what to have for dinner. This may not seem like a big deal, but to me it was: it helped me learn how to act on what I wanted.

I'd mentioned going back to school before, but although this was something I desperately wanted, there always seemed to be reasons for me not to do it. Now, having gained a new sense of independence,

I was able to pursue my dream of continuing my education.

On the evening of October 31, I was texting with Tony, and he explained that he was concerned about some things. He was no longer sure that we had the same goals, and he was wondering where he fit into my life. He had always wanted a simple life, while I wanted to travel, to see the world, to have a life of excitement and adventure.

Then, he made a statement which chilled me to the bone. He said, "I feel that I am holding you back. Perhaps God does not want us to be together anymore."

He went on to say that said that he realized he was not in a position to give me the life I wanted—a life he had no desire to live. He felt that I would be more able to focus on what I wanted if I did not have to worry about him.

I was devastated. I was thirty-six, and we had been married for almost eighteen years—half my life. I had never expected that something like this could happen. I had no idea what I was going to do. Those voices exploded in my head, telling me I was a failure, and that my life was over.

I called my best friend, SueAnn, crying like a baby. I cried myself to sleep that night, and stayed in bed for most of the next day.

I did not talk to Tony again until the following Monday. When, instead of acting regretful, he had the same nonchalant attitude, I finally found the courage to tell the voices in my head to shut up. It was as though God had flipped a switch in my mind.

Calm for the first time in days, I was able to tell Tony that I agreed with him. He *had* been holding me back, and I wanted a divorce. Then, I would be free to make decisions based on the desires of my heart. I could focus on God and follow His direction without Tony's influence.

The paperwork was filed on November 13th, and on December 2nd—the day after my birthday—I was officially divorced.

The excitement and liberation I feel now is so amazing. The voices in my head have not gone away, but I am tremendously pleased to say that with God's help, I am quicker to tell them to be quiet. I am learning that I need to be myself, and stop wishing to be like other people. If I do that, I will miss out on being me—and after all, I am the only one who is qualified for that job. I have also realized that I cannot be perfect, no matter how hard I try: perfection is God's department.

Most importantly, finding my passion has helped me to understand that while my family, my job, and my friends are important, my life is too short to lose who I am, and who God has intended me to be.

Prior to my divorce, I knew that I wanted to be a writer and speaker, but I was never able to push past my doubts, fears, and anxieties to pursue that goal. While I often toyed with the idea of writing, it was hard to be creative while worrying that my partner wouldn't be happy with my decision to be creative. Now, I've finally decided what I want to be when I grow up, and I've taken steps to pursue that goal on a larger scale.

By depending only on God, I have come to realize that I can do anything through Him, because He strengthens me. I have been reading anything and everything I can about the craft of writing, listening and watching for God's guidance. During an incredible Bible study on freedom and God's promises, I realized that I needed to write about my experience with fear so I could share my story with other women.

Just a few days later, I came across Linda Joy, and was granted the opportunity to be part of this book.

When you focus on God, and ask in faith for the desires of your heart, it is wondrous what He will do!

Juicy Questions

Does this story speak to you? The journaling prompts below can help you access messages from your authentic core, and integrate the richness and insights of this story into your own juicy, joyful life!

What do you want to be "when you grow up?"

_____

_____

_____

If you're feeling stifled or frustrated in the area of that goal, what do you think is holding you back? Like Dianna, could you be holding *yourself* back, without even realizing it?

_____

_____

_____

Before her divorce, Dianna couldn't imagine life without her husband—but that separation was necessary to help her realize her goals. Sometimes, the things that hurt us most are the things which allow us to realize our true potential. When has this been true in your life?

_____

_____

_____

The Safe Path

Amy Beth O'Brien

What is it that causes us to ignore our gifts, suppress our desires, shrug off our talents, and pursue lives as plain as white toast? How did this come to be perceived as the "safe" path?

I led much of my life this way, until a strong urge to write came upon me while I was figuring out how to end a relationship. Joe told me I was lucky to have him because I was a single mother and, "Not many men would take that on." He encouraged me to give up the idea of starting my own business to stay in my boring but reliable state job. I knew I wanted to live a more creative life—a life full of the sweet stuff—but it would mean going it alone, this time for real, and that was terribly intimidating.

Writing was an urge I couldn't explain. I tried to push it away. After all, I wasn't a "real" writer. Growing up, Judy Blume novels were my favorite. I loved the *Anne of Green Gables* stories. "If only I could write like Lucy Maud Montgomery," I thought. But "real" writers...Real writers held degrees in fine arts; they had agents and publishers. They followed a specific path that usually began with a parent-teacher conference.

I imagined a scene that went something like this:

"Your child is gifted," the teacher gushed. The parents smiled knowingly at one another, then gazed lovingly at the little protégé sitting between them. The teacher recommend advanced placement. The child went to an Ivy League college on a full scholarship, and finished her first novel by the time she was twenty-five. The End.

My teachers never identified any special talent in me. I never fell in love with the classics. I hadn't even finished *Anna Karenina*. I simply wasn't that person; therefore, the idea that I could write was nonsensical.

Instead, I picked up a pair of knitting needles. When I was nine, I'd felt inexplicably drawn to my Great Aunt Frieda's colorful yarns and gorgeous hand-made sweaters. I sat on her living room sofa as she patiently taught me to knit and purl. But by the time I was ten, I'd learned that only old ladies knit, not young girls. Family members poked fun at me, so I worked clandestinely in my bedroom.

Now, as an adult, knitting somehow seemed safe. Writing was the new, forbidden fruit.

As mittens, hats, and sweaters went to delighted friends and family members, I developed a technique for dealing with my relationship with Joe which emboldened me. I started looking at my life as though it were a movie. I decided that I wanted to be an inspirational character, not a frustrating victim who couldn't get out of her own way. I began to assert myself. No longer willing to play best supporting actress, molding myself to another person's tastes, I became the star of my own life story.

I wrote down what I wanted in a home, how I wanted it to feel, and how I wanted our lives to be. I established my own career coaching business, and did a little editing work. I removed the things from my life that held me back—including my relationship. I started over in a new community with my two young boys.

The stage was set for a new life, in which I was the heroine. But my writing was still hovering in the background, like a child with stage fright.

I was walking along the Charles River one day when I realized I couldn't hold back any longer. I had a conversation going on inside my head about the time I found my ex-husband at another woman's apartment; I had moved on, but I hadn't gotten over it. The voices in my head turned into characters in a movie, and those voices flowed out of me like a tsunami. I felt everything shift, and suddenly, nothing could stop my inner writer. Since I saw the story as a motion picture, I started working on a screenplay.

It wasn't the first time I'd honored a calling. That inner urging was what drew me to become a trainer, a mother, and a yoga instructor. But writers still seemed almost otherworldly to me. It's not that I didn't write at all: I received positive feedback on my newsletter articles and training programs. But that was business, not personal. It was nothing that could expose me.

I kept my script a secret, working on it on nights and weekends, until one day I met a "real" writer. Hundreds of books adorned his shelves. His sense of humor left me in stitches. I thought I'd met a kindred spirit, although I couldn't put my finger on what it was about him that drew me. He'd followed the prescribed path, the one I'd always envisioned. He'd attended an Ivy League college on a full scholarship. He'd completed his first novel at twenty-five.

In the face of his story, I was almost ashamed to admit I had such lofty aspirations. To me, my writing still wasn't real; I was just playing at it. Telling myself it was just a hobby allowed me to give it a try.

When I finally felt brave enough to tell Mr. Real Writer about my screenplay, he said, "Thirty-nine year old women from Massachusetts don't write screenplays. I'm the star here, not you."

I felt myself begin to shrivel up like a raisin, disintegrating, sinking into the earth. I stood up and grabbed my purse with all the dignity I could muster. "See ya!" I said to Mr. Real, peppering my remarks with a few four letter words as I stormed out of his apartment. What a load of crap!

I knew he wasn't right about me. After all, I was the star of my own life story. I decided who I wanted to be, and what I wanted to do. I couldn't allow other people's hang-ups and insecurities to keep me from my dreams. I realized then that the people I'd attracted—Joe, Mr. Real—were simply mirrors of my own inner critic. After that day, I finally put them, and her, in their place.

Somewhere along the way, we've come to believe that all vocations are akin to becoming an Olympic athlete—that we have to start in preschool, and finish by the time we're forty—but these rules aren't real. Our dreams call to us. They are the urges, signs, and intuitive signals that say, "Pick up that paint brush. Take those ballroom dance lessons. Buy the shiny, blue electric guitar you've been admiring. Go! Do it!" Theirs are the inner voices of authenticity—the voices of the real you, who waits patiently to be born.

All along, I'd encouraged my coaching clients to pursue their dreams, but it wasn't until I started writing that I paid the same respect to myself. My education and life experiences prepared me for the writing and speaking I was meant to do. My work as a trainer and coach taught me the mechanics. My relationships and studies gave me the material. In order to write, I needed to complete the first leg of my journey.

It took time for me to honor my inner artist, but it helped me to honor others' stories as well—to write about them, and to be a guide for them along their path. I finished my screenplay, and I'm now a blogger, an author, a coach, and a speaker, helping other women star in their own life stories.

Fear causes us to ignore our gifts, suppress our desires, and shrug off our talents. Fear is what drives us to stay on the "safe" path—the path of white toast, the path of nothing special. Choose instead to pursue your dreams. Move forward with faith that if you play full-out, honor your inner artist, and do what you love, you will find the *only* safe path: the path of truth.

That's what living a juicy, joyful life is all about.

Juicy Questions

Does this story speak to you? The journaling prompts below can help you access messages from your authentic core, and integrate the richness and insights of this story into your own juicy, joyful life!

Is there something you've always wanted to do, but are afraid you're not "qualified" to pursue?

_____

_____

_____

_____

Are there people in your life who mirror the voice of your inner critic? How can you begin to shift these relationships so that they feel more supportive and nurturing?

_____

_____

_____

_____

When in your life have you followed a calling? Did you regret doing so? When have you ignored a calling in favor of the "safe" path? Do you regret this?

_____

_____

_____

_____

L.I.F.E.

Nancy Olsen

I have had a heaviness in my gut for as long as I can remember, a feeling that life is too short; that I need to see and experience everything this world has to offer before it's too late.

This feeling fueled in me a sense of urgency which resulted in numerous relocations across the globe. I was never going to look back on my life and wonder, "What if?" I was going to take chances. I was going to savor every place I visited, and every culture I encountered.

Where did this feeling originate? Was I running to something, or away from something? I didn't know.

My family and I moved from Chicago to San Francisco in September, 2008. Who would choose to move their three-year-old and eight-month-old sons 1,200 miles from their closest relatives? Well... we would! My husband and I had decided very early on that we would not live a life of missed opportunities. We were going to follow our dreams, and have faith in the man up above that we were on the right path. Without words to explain it, we knew in our hearts that California was where we were supposed to be.

A couple of months later, my parents came to visit for Thanksgiving. I sensed during that visit that something was not right. You know that feeling—the one where your gut tells you something is wrong, but you can't put your finger on what it is. My mom was scheduled for a preventative oophorectomy the following week; her sister had been diagnosed with stage IV ovarian cancer twelve years earlier. A routine surgery, the specialists called it—but events were soon to reveal a different story.

The night before I got the news, I had a dream. I saw my mom sitting in a hospital bed, wearing a white gown. Her doctor gave me her chart to read. Under the lab results, her diagnosis was written.

I awoke abruptly, knowing full well what my body had been trying to tell me a week earlier. My mother had cancer.

The next day started like any other. The boys woke my husband and me (no need for alarm clocks with those two); I got dressed, corralled my guys for breakfast, checked in with our nanny, and started my day. My dad was scheduled to call later that morning to let me know how my mom's surgery had gone—but I didn't need a call. I already knew.

My dad phoned around 9:30 a.m. When I answered, the first words out of my mouth were "I know, Dad."

"How do you know?"

I didn't tell him about the dream. "What stage?" I asked.

"Three."

Although I'd prepared myself to hear them, those words hit me like a bomb. Stage III ovarian cancer? How could this happen? Since my aunt's diagnosis, my mom had been diligent about receiving regular check-ups. How could the doctors not have found this sooner?

I spent the following weeks partly disbelieving, partly mourning the loss of someone I had yet to lose. How could I face life without my mother? Who would be there to listen to me, support me, and rejoice with me through the years to come? Would my boys remember all she did for them, how she loved them? I knew the statistics, but my aunt was a survivor. Like her sister, my mom would—must—also beat the odds!

Soon, my grief turned to anger. I didn't need this lesson in my life. I already knew how precious life was, how each day is a gift! I had been living in the moment, truly experiencing life, ever since I could remember: traveling the world, meeting people, seeing new things.

Or had I?

After the anger came the fear. I wondered what my mother's diagnosis meant for me. What were my risks? I talked to my doctor, but the surgical preventative measures offered seemed quite extreme. How long could I wait? How aggressive was I willing to be, surgically and otherwise, in the name of prevention? How far was I willing to go to potentially save my own life? In the midst of my mother's trial, I was forced to confront my ultimate fear—my own mortality. Life was too short already, and now I was staring into the crystal ball, wondering if my future was going to get even shorter.

I took a critical look at my own life. Was I truly experiencing each and every moment, or did I just exist day to day? I realized that I was caught up in the daily rigors of life, trying to juggle my multiple roles as wife, mother, and driven career woman simultaneously. Too many times, I realized, these roles rolled into one. I was losing my spark— that glow in me that lets the world know I'm here, and that I'm a force to be reckoned with. Trying to live to the fullest, I had lost my passion for life. I was constantly on the move, but all the while I was running away from my own fear.

In an instant, a weight was lifted. That unnamed heaviness no longer weighed on my heart. Was this really what I'd been running from?

My mom's diagnosis was my mental wake-up call. When a loved one gets a second chance in life, you can't help but see your own life through a different lens. We traveled her road to recovery together, and after the dust settled, I lit a fire under myself. I burned more brightly than ever. I took back the reins of my life. I didn't know what the future held, but I knew that I was going to live with a passion that was off the charts! Instead of continuing to live in a state of wanting— wanting to do more, see more, be more—I chose to focus on what was already in my life that made me happy.

I tell this story in the hopes that you won't need a traumatic wake-up call to start living the life God gave you. Instead of thinking about what you don't have, find the things in your life that escalate your energy level, and bring that energy to each and every moment of your day. It's the Law of Attraction: like attracts like. Don't just exist day to day. Exist with a passion that's immeasurable, and L-I-F-E—*Let It Feel Exhilarating!*

Juicy Questions

Does this story speak to you? The journaling prompts below can help you access messages from your authentic core, and integrate the richness and insights of this story into your own juicy, joyful life!

Would your life be better or more complete if you only _____ ? (You fill in the blank)

_____

_____

_____

Nancy felt the constant need to do more, see more, and be more because she harbored a deep fear of her own mortality. What fears or questions drive you to search for more than you have now?

_____

_____

_____

What aspects of the experiences you crave are already present in your life? How can you explore them further, and bring their joy into each day?

_____

_____

_____

_____

Straight from the Heart

Roseanne Masone

S ometimes, it takes an unexpected turn of events to push us in the direction we really want to go. The added impetus we gain brings us to the realization that we actually can make deliberate changes in our thinking, and in turn, our day-to-day lives. In my case, the "push" was a dramatic, frightening, and life-altering experience.

It all started on a sub-zero Sunday morning in January, some six years ago. My husband and I, both avid skiers, headed to a nearby mountain for a much-needed day of fresh air, exercise, and fun. Midway down one of our favorite ski runs, I felt an odd pain in my right arm and across my throat. I stopped and rested for a moment, and the discomfort stopped. We both thought it could be a reaction to breathing in the extreme cold—but as we continued the run, the pain returned, so we slowly made our way back to the ski lodge. I was scared and confused. I wondered if I was having a heart attack, but all the things I'd read about heart attacks didn't seem to apply here. I didn't have shortness of breath, and the pain was in my right arm and upper chest, not my left arm.

Once we sat down at the lodge, I felt better, but we decided to leave for home anyway. My husband wanted to stop at a local emergency room, but since I was feeling better, I told him no, I'd just call my doctor first thing in the morning.

That night and the next morning I still felt fine, but I was perplexed by my previous symptoms. After all, I exercised regularly and watched my diet. I felt I was, for all practical purposes, healthy. There was no reason I should be experiencing pain like that.

The doctor's visit seemed to confirm my belief. The exam, which included an EKG, showed nothing abnormal. But to be on the safe side, she scheduled me for a stress test three days later—the earliest appointment available, considering that this was not an emergency.

The next morning, I went to my office as usual, still feeling okay. Once there, however, I started to feel discomfort again, and this time it was worse. I was really scared. A colleague called for an ambulance, and off I went to the hospital. As I lay there on the stretcher, with the ambulance's sirens blaring overhead, I couldn't believe what was happening. I was healthy! How could this be?

Luckily, a cardiologist happened to be in the ER that day. He quickly discovered that I had a blocked coronary artery. A clot-busting drug relieved the heart attack—yes, I'd been having a heart attack—but I needed a stent to ensure that the artery would remain open.

I was transferred to another hospital which was licensed by the state to perform stent procedures. The operation was successful, and I was sent home to recuperate.

As it turned out, the heart attack was the least of my worries. During the stent procedure, I was exposed to a staph infection that didn't surface for several weeks. When it did, I found myself literally fighting for my life. The infection was focused in my heart and my left leg. I developed endocarditis, my leg was grotesquely swollen and covered with red sores, and my kidneys started to shut down. Quick thinking and emergency surgery saved my leg and my life, but I was left with a leg that had vascular damage and atrophied muscles.

Determined to get my life back as quickly as possible, I began a regimen of physical therapy and exercise along with intravenous antibiotic therapy. My husband and I had planned a trip to Bonaire before my heart attack, and I was determined to be well enough to go. The doctor said that if I regained sufficient strength in my leg and my heart infection was gone, I could dive again in five months. I kept a photo of me scuba diving by my bedside for inspiration.

While at home recovering, I resumed my nutritional program, which included protein shakes and supplements sanctioned by my doctor. I was severely anemic due to hemorrhaging and had required two pints of blood during my hospital stay. I started out slowly, since I'd lost about twenty pounds and my stomach had shrunk considerably, but day by day, I felt my strength coming back.

At the same time, I decided to undertake some emotional healing as well. I had always been spiritual, and life had now presented me with the perfect opportunity to expand my thinking. I listened to inspirational CDs over and over again, and began applying the principles I heard.

Over and over, I repeated to myself that I was healed, and that I was deeply grateful for that healing. I had always had a strong faith, but now I relied on it more than ever before. I visualized diving again, and having a wonderful time doing so. My physical limitations were not going to drag me down.

I started out using one foot at a time to climb the stairs to our bedroom. It would take forever to go up and down, and my left leg hurt terribly. After relatively little effort, I felt exhausted, as if I had exercised for hours. Each step was a painful reminder of what I had been through, and even the simplest things were a challenge, but I persevered, truly believing it was possible to achieve my goal. I wanted to dive again, so I needed a strong heart. I wanted to ski again, so I needed two strong legs. I continually visualized myself doing both of those things with a smile on my face, and remained grateful for every new day, because every new day was a new chance. I *deserved* to be healthy and happy, and therefore I would be!

I didn't look back, and I didn't spend time wondering, "Why me?" When negative thoughts invaded my mind, I took control and changed the subject. I knew that if I took my cues from my current situation, I would simply generate more negative and fearful feelings, which would translate into negative physical results. Instead, I stayed focused on my goals, and reminded myself that I actually had a say in how I felt and how fast I could heal. Beliefs, after all, are only thoughts we keep thinking. Simply being grateful for what I had opened doors to what I wanted most. I found that when I felt genuinely grateful, more of what I wanted came to me. I was grateful to be alive, and my life began to come back to me. That, in turn, brought me even more things to be grateful for.

After a long recovery, I did take that trip to Bonaire, and eventually healed completely. Today I remain in excellent health and

149

continue to scuba dive, ski, horseback ride, bicycle, and more. I'm truly enjoying my life to the fullest.

We are surrounded by things that can make us happy every day—a flower, a rainbow, or a memory of a favorite experience. Find your happiness within, and from the things around you, and let it shine as your beacon to attract even more happiness. If you take your cues for life straight from the heart, you can't go wrong!

Juicy Questions

Does this story speak to you? The journaling prompts below can help you access messages from your authentic core, and integrate the richness and insights of this story into your own juicy, joyful life!

We all have challenges in our lives. Some, like Rosanne's, are physical; others are emotional. How have you reacted to the challenges in your life thus far?

_____

_____

_____

When you fall into a pattern of negative thinking, it's easy to attract more negativity. Has this ever happened to you? Were you able to turn your thoughts around?

_____

_____

_____

If you're in the midst of a challenge right now, how can you change your thought process to affect the outcome? What can you choose to be grateful for right now?

_____

_____

_____

_____

FAITH, LOVE,
AND *Devotion*

Good Medicine

Joy Earle

It took me a while to learn how to swallow a pill when I was a kid. It took even longer for me to learn to take a healthy dose of Joyful Heart as medicine. A joyful heart isn't something you get in one shot, either. It's a daily dose for what ails ya!

I want to share with you a story of medicinal joy.

In 1982, I was twenty-four years old, and living in South Florida. I'd just left my home in Louisville, Kentucky to be near my family—and quite honestly, to find a man! In Louisville, I'd watched almost every friend I had get married, and felt like it was my turn to do the same.

My parents mentioned that I might get involved with the young adult stuff at church to make some friends. At their suggestion, I volunteered to sing one night at an event that included local music and bands. In the back of my mind, I hoped that there would be a handsome man there who loved music too!

I walked into the fellowship hall and looked around for a friendly face. I met some really nice people, and was encouraged by their kindness to me—but more than anything, I wanted to find someone to spend time (and perhaps my life) with. Well, I looked up again, and there he was: Mr. Right. His name was Jeff. We had an immediate connection, and after a brief conversation I learned that not only did Jeff love music, he was a musician. Jackpot!

I got to know Jeff better, and I prayed every day that God would give Jeff to me. I felt that I was the logical choice for him, so we should just get this show on the road. But although Jeff and I got along just fine, God wasn't quick to hand him over.

I had always been told God had a plan for my life, but God wasn't moving fast enough, so I decided to give Him some help. And boy oh boy, did I make a mess of it! I pretty much threw myself at poor Jeff, and did all the things we tell our daughters not to do! I strategically placed myself where I knew he would be. I didn't stalk the guy, or follow him home, but I *really* wanted him to want me.

My dream died the day Jeff told me that we would always be friends. He liked being friends, he said, and he didn't want that to change. In short, he didn't want me the way I wanted him. My little-girl dream had been simple: fall in love, get married, make a house a home, raise a family with lots of love and laughter. Now, the rug had been pulled out from underneath me, and I didn't have a backup dream. I was suddenly facing my greatest fear: being alone.

I wallowed in my fear for a while, convinced that I would never have what other women my age had, and that I would be alone forever. This went on until one afternoon, while lying by the pool, I finally took a long look at where my life's journey had brought me. I admitted to myself that sulking wasn't going to help me the least little bit. Neither was eating a whole bag of Oreo cookies, and topping it off with a pint of ice cream! There were choices to be made, and I needed a revelation.

I chose to have a joyful heart—a revelation of love from the one who loved me the most. I had never stopped to contemplate a future with just me in it, but why did I think that was such a bad thing?

The power surge in my heart that day freed me to chase my dreams for myself with as much determination as I had chased Jeff. I filled my life with activities that had nothing to do with finding a mate. I focused on my talents, one of which was music. I accepted an invitation to sing at a coffee house in town, and it was like a premiere of sorts. After that, I was asked to sing at weddings and events all over town—and they were payin' real money! I volunteered several days a week after work at the retirement villages, entertaining the old folks. I went canoeing, fishing, and even tried water skiing (I hated it).

Best of all, I started noticing the people I had ignored while on my quest for the perfect man. I found so many interesting souls full of warmth, information and fun. I rented a house with three friends, and although we all had separate lives, we shared a common bond of friendship and loyalty. It was a wonderful experience, and we had so much fun! Saturday mornings, still in our flannel gowns after sleeping fashionably late, we would dance around with candle sticks in our hands, lip-syncing our favorite songs.

I went shopping for new clothes that expressed who I was. It was hilarious—remember, this was the 1980s! I love bright colors and unique designs, so I bought some for myself and set a trend in town. My big hair, once forsaken for the Florida heat, came back as well. I had to spend a little more on hairspray, but who cared? I was happy!

My life, once an ordinary piece of music, was now a symphony, with all of the instruments playing in perfect time with one another. I sang high notes of confidence and courage that had never been sung in my heart before, and they were perfectly in tune with me, and where I was going. I embraced life for what it was, and gave up on trying to change things that were beyond my control. And (hold on to your hats!) I even allowed myself to be Jeff's friend. Jeff dated some really cute girls, but I no longer felt like the last one picked for kickball, because I was captain of my own team! I dated some very nice young men, and some not so nice, but I was also very happy to not date at all. It was just as much fun spending time with me.

157

I wouldn't trade those two years of growth and self-discovery for anything. I had an awakening in my spirit, and was no longer afraid to love God with my whole heart, soul, and mind. I stopped micromanaging my life and let Him call the shots. I took chances, and made mistakes, but I wasn't afraid anymore. I knew I would be safe on my life's journey because I was only along for the ride! I had finally grown up and there was no turning back.

People are not designed to perfectly meet someone else's needs, or complete someone else's life. People are designed to enjoy the life that only God can live, and the love that only God can give. I started swallowing my daily dose of Joyful Heart years ago, and I will never discontinue my prescription: in fact, I'm on automatic refill! I found my inner giggle, and a smile of deep contentment in spite of my everyday circumstance.

Are you wondering what happened to good ole' Jeff? Well, I am happy to report that we are still friends—even after twenty-five years of marriage! We fell in love the right way. After I learned to love myself as much as I loved him, God gave us to each other. Jeff will tell you that he has a wife with big hair, a bigger mouth, and an even bigger appetite for laughter and fun. The symphony plays, and the two of us sing along in perfect harmony.

Girls, take your medicine!

Juicy Questions

Does this story speak to you? The journaling prompts below can help you access messages from your authentic core, and integrate the richness and insights of this story into your own juicy, joyful life!

Sometimes the things we want most are not right for us at this moment in time. In order to truly succeed in her relationship with Jeff, Joy first had to learn to love herself. Has your heart's greatest desire ever been deferred or denied? What lessons did you learn because of it?

_____

_____

_____

Often, our fears tell us where we need to work to create the best, happiest versions of ourselves. When Joy conquered her fear of being alone, she transformed her life and discovered her Joyful Heart. What is your greatest fear? How can you work toward overcoming it in a positive, empowering way?

_____

_____

_____

What does a Joyful Heart mean to you? How can you integrate a daily dose of your own "medicine" into your life?

_____

_____

_____

Two Soulmates, One Lifetime

Kathleen Sims

When I was sixteen years old, I was sitting in the high school cafeteria with my girlfriend when a couple of guys walked in. They caught my attention immediately. I asked my friend if she knew the one in the suit; she didn't.

"I'm going to go out with him," I told her. The words gave me a jolt; I didn't even recognize them as my own.

A moment later, a vivid picture came into my mind. I saw myself married to that dark-haired guy, living in suburbia with two kids, a dog, and a white picket fence. Not only did I see this, I *felt* it, as surely as if it had already happened. Linear time had disappeared, and in that moment, I was living the future.

"Actually," I said, "I'm going to marry him."

Needless to say, my friend was speechless. Looking back, I can hardly believe it myself. But after that day, I committed to my vision of the future with bold behavior and confidence to match. I made sure I was in every hall that dark-haired guy walked down. I hung out near his car. I got his friend to set us up on a first date. He didn't have a chance—not that he wanted one.

And the rest, as they say, is history.

A year later, Jim and I were married, with a baby on the way. We'd already purchased our own home, complete with a white picket fence. I wasn't even eighteen years old. Everyone told us it would never last; we were too young, they said. But I already knew how things would turn out. The knowledge had been bestowed upon me by something greater than myself.

I didn't immediately admit to Jim what prompted my pursuit of him: I was afraid he would think I was crazy, or that he hadn't had any choice in the matter. But fifteen years later, when I finally found the nerve to tell him about my clairvoyant experience in the high school cafeteria, he only nodded and said, "That's interesting, because the first time I met your mother, I had the strangest feeling. I didn't recognize it at the time, but I couldn't sleep for three nights after that. I felt like I knew her intimately, but I'd never met her before." It was obvious, Jim and I agreed, that there were divine forces at work in our relationship.

As our lives unfolded, the questions seemed more and more significant. How had this happened to us? Had we created our love for ourselves, or was there something more at work? Could others learn to duplicate our experience? After years of meditating, praying, reading, and listening, I discovered that there were in fact certain principles at play in our lives, and that they were teachable to anyone.

I understood then that this knowledge had come to me for a reason larger than my own happiness. It was for me to use, and give away. Jim's and my purpose together had been revealed at last: we were to be a model for love and learning in the world, because in the presence of love all are touched. I created a program to teach others how to bring deep, abiding love into their lives, and Jim stepped forward to take care of everything around me—the kids, the house, the dog—serving and nurturing us all so I would be free to teach what we'd learned. I spoke alone to rooms full of people, but it was as if Jim was there beside me the entire time.

For nearly four decades, Jim and I interacted in what I call a "relationship Petri dish," exploring our greatest questions. How much love can we give and receive in a lifetime? What makes love diminish, and what makes it deepen? I won't say we didn't push each others' buttons, and there were some very challenging issues, but through it all we stood strong on the unshakable foundation of our love and our eternal connection.

One Sunday morning, Jim stopped me in the hall, and enfolded me in a long, sweet hug. "Everyone is yearning for this kind of love and connection, Kathleen," he said to me. "And most people don't even know it exists."

Those were the last words he ever said to me. Thirty minutes later, he suffered a sudden heart attack, and was gone.

I was in shock. Being married to Jim was all I knew, all I'd ever known. I thought I would never know love like that again—that I'd been given this tremendous gift, and now it had been taken away.

But two and a half years later, having processed my grief and transformed my self-identity, I was able to apply the same principles to my own life that I'd spend years teaching to others. I looked at my beliefs, healed my misconceptions, and let go of the old, finally forgiving the loss of Jim. Then, having completed my inner homework, I decided I was ready for a new research project. What, I wondered, was it like to be single at sixty?

Dating was a whole new world for me—after all, I'd never done it. I wondered, how did dating work these days? Where could one meet nice men?

My research indicated that online dating was the way to go, so I rolled up my sleeves and got started, determined to learn on the fast track. In six months, I interfaced with over two hundred men, and met about thirty.

After a number of great (and not-so-great) dating experiences, it happened again.

After only two e-mails with a new gentleman, we set a date and location to meet face-to-face. I was breaking all my own rules—no phone call, no prior contact—but I had a strong intuitive sense that I was supposed to say "Yes."

On the way to the restaurant, fear caught up with me. I hadn't done my due diligence; what if this was a bad idea? But my hesitation was quickly washed away by a wave of calm as a voice in my head whispered, "Trust the process."

I walked into the restaurant, and there he was. He reached out and gave me a warm hug—and there *it* was, an intense vibration of familiarity and recognition, a knowing that ignited my entire being. I hadn't even heard his voice, yet our souls had already established a connection beyond words. I put my hands on his shoulders, looked into his eyes, and said, "Oh, my gosh! It's you!"

Needless to say, he was baffled. "I hope I like this man," I thought, as we walked to our table. "Because I'm going to be with him for a long time!" The evening unfolded in a magical way, and we discovered that our passions, priorities, and values were in perfect alignment. I recognized the divine gift which had been bestowed upon me once again, and embraced it.

Bob and I had the adventures of a lifetime. He taught me how to snow ski, fly his airplane, and drive his race car. In turn, I taught him about unconditional love, and how two people can use a relationship as a spiritual path. We were inseparable, and our lives wove together like a perfect tapestry.

One Monday, we went to dinner. He called on Tuesday to express how delightful the night before had been for him. On Wednesday, we didn't have a chance to chat, but I wasn't concerned.

At 4:00 p.m. on Thursday, I was standing in my office when I felt an electric jolt go through my body, like I'd been shocked. It scared me a bit, but it passed quickly, and when it didn't happen again, I decided not to think about it.

I called Bob that night, and every day for the next three days. He didn't answer, nor did he call me back, which was very strange. On Monday morning, I opened my e-mail to find a message from Bob's daughter. "Call me," it read.

When she answered the phone, she said, simply, "Dad is gone."

Bob had been flying his best friend to a funeral in Utah when he'd been caught in a blizzard in the Ruby Mountains. At 4:00 p.m. on Thursday, his wings iced over, and he missed the top of a mountain by five hundred feet.

I was speechless. I remembered the electric shock I'd felt on that fateful Thursday, and now I knew it was the explosion of Bob's plane on the mountainside. I cried for days, asking God, "Why Bob? He was such a perfect mate for me!"

After long hours of prayer and contemplation, I still didn't have an answer, but I was suddenly awash in an intense feeling of gratitude. My heart was so full. I'd been blessed to be loved by two very special men, and although they were gone, their love for me remained in my heart. Nothing inside me was missing.

I have experienced two miracles of deep, abiding love in my life— one at sixteen, and one at sixty. Today, I continue to live aware of the fullness within me, and have lots of joyful memories to make me smile. I'm doing my inner homework again, and soon I know I will be ready to attract another soul mate into my life, because there is always the possibility of love in God's plan for us.

Juicy Questions

Does this story speak to you? The journaling prompts below can help you access messages from your authentic core, and integrate the richness and insights of this story into your own juicy, joyful life!

Have you ever felt something so strongly that you just knew it would come true? Was this thing positive or negative? How did you react to your knowing?

_____

_____

_____

_____

Kathleen met two soul mates in her lifetime. Do you believe that you've experienced soul mate love?

_____

_____

_____

_____

How much love do you believe a person can give and receive in a lifetime? Are you giving and receiving love at this capacity? How can you open your heart to the love that exists within you and around you?

_____

_____

_____

_____

Tapped on the Shoulder

Kris Steinnes

One day, not so very long ago, I attended a lecture at Seattle Unity Church. I was waiting in the pew for the program to begin, when I saw the program director walking up the aisle on the other side of the church to attend the speaker. All of a sudden, a Voice spoke to me. "That will be your job someday," it said.

At the time, I didn't give it much thought. I just said to myself, "Well, that's interesting," and turned my attention back to the speaker.

Five years later, I did get that job. It was as though I was destined to have it. Reflecting on this now, I would say that the Voice I heard that day came from somewhere behind me, not within me. I had no preconceived thoughts before I heard it that might have led me to think the words which were spoken. I wasn't dreaming or conjecturing.

My story goes further back than that day—to the day when I first found Unity Church, and began my journey towards my life purpose.

My husband and I returned to Seattle in 1986 after traveling around the world for three years. I was feeling the need to pursue a spiritual path, and soon discovered Unity Church and the programs they had to offer.

Soon, I became obsessive about attending church every week, and for six months I cried at every service. I remember wondering when I would be able to attend a service *without* shedding tears. Now I know that I was feeding my soul, refilling my spirit after years without a spiritual home.

I attended church every week while I was growing up, but it wasn't by my own choice, and by the time I reached my late teens I began to rebel, finding all sorts of excuses for why I wasn't able to go. In college, I continued to shy away, preferring to go to the library to work on homework. I felt trapped in my traditional religion, where

I heard only the fear of God and His punishment. That just didn't fit my image of what God was.

What I didn't recognize until recently was that I couldn't relate to my childhood church or the services there because the feminine voice was absent. I couldn't see myself, a young woman, in the church's expression of God. It wasn't the religion itself, but rather the heavy voice of the patriarchy, that I rebelled against in my youth. Only two decades later, when I found Unity Church, was I able to feel the love of God, and the love of an accepting community, in a church setting.

Even before I found Unity Church, I heard that Voice in my head. One day, when I was a teen, I was sitting on the sofa, staring out our front window. I remember looking at the tress, and then hearing someone say, "You'll do something important in your fifties." As I didn't feel like I fit in to the social cliques at school, it was comforting to hear this, and I didn't question it, or ask how this would come to be.

Another piece of knowledge came to me in 1989. It came through another person, not out of thin air, but it struck me so profoundly that I knew I was hearing the voice of God. We were on a Unity retreat, and Danaan Parry, founder of Peace Trees Vietnam and a global leader in people-to-people diplomacy, was leading a workshop. In a room full of more than five hundred people and chairs, we were blindfolded, and asked to wander around and bump into people. When we found a partner, we were to speak our purpose to that person.

I said, "I am going to bring people together." I'd made this statement before, in another workshop, but I hadn't yet acted upon it. My partner, having witnessed my purpose, repeated it back to me as though I were already doing it: "You are bringing people together."

The impact of this was so strong for me that, when we were told to separate and remove our blindfolds, I couldn't move. I sat in silence for ten minutes, reeling from the shock of it. The voice my partner had spoken with was not a human voice, and the message was not a human message. I had heard the voice of God, confirming my purpose to me.

I knew what I was meant to do, but it still took several more years to realize how my purpose would unfold. In 1992, I read *The Feminine Face of God* by Patricia Hopkins and Sherry Anderson, and soon after received another message from the Voice, this time on a late-night drive. "Bring spiritual women leaders to Unity so that you may experience their stories in person." Then, it got more specific: "Create a one week conference. Create a community of women." It was as though God had tapped me on the shoulder, and said, "It's time!"

And so, my mission was founded in 1993. Women of Wisdom has become one of the longest-running spiritual conferences in the country.

My most recent encounter with the Voice came while I was giving a one-hour workshop on leadership. I had completed our agenda with ten minutes to spare, so I decided to share my concept of Circle Leadership, which is how the Women of Wisdom Foundation is managed. A man in my group was very excited, and said, "This is a new paradigm! You need to write a book, go on Oprah!"

Of course, I was pleased at his response—but what he said wasn't as important as the picture his words opened up in my mind. In that moment, I saw a larger vision for my mission. I wasn't only going to bring people together; I was going to be a voice to raise the feminine consciousness within all of us.

I like to share my experiences with the Voice so that others can see how little revelations can lead to larger and more important developments in our lives. I heard things, yes, but the changes they inspired didn't happen overnight. Anyone can create their life's purpose one step at a time, as long as they listen closely when that Voice speaks. I didn't set out to create this life; rather, it unfolded as I discovered more about myself and my life's work.

This year I claimed a new mission, and stated a new purpose: I am the Expression of the Divine Feminine. This is very important for me, and challenging as well: this is something I need to embody, not just talk about. As I become this expression, others will see the value of the Divine Feminine in me, and come to respect and cherish it. All too often, we close ourselves off to this aspect of ourselves, having learned through generations to ignore it. This isn't about gender; it's a message for men and women both. When we operate solely from our masculine nature, it's almost like trying to live with half our body missing. There's no way to find balance when half of your self is gone.

When I witness women finding the courage to express themselves, I am filled with joy. In moments of discovery, we are blessed by each others' growth. When each of us expands into the person we truly are, the collective consciousness shifts. We're not just moving through our personal journeys; we are cultivating the evolution of humanity.

Juicy Questions

Does this story speak to you? The journaling prompts below can help you access messages from your authentic core, and integrate the richness and insights of this story into your own juicy, joyful life!

Have you ever heard a voice speaking to you out of thin air, as Kris did? Did you listen to it? Ignore it? What changes did it inspire?

_____

_____

_____

_____

Do you have a personal mission?

_____

_____

_____

_____

Are you currently working to fulfill your personal mission? If not, what steps can you take to embody it?

_____

_____

_____

_____

Maintain Your Identity, Keep Your Sanity

Crystal Willms

Have you ever had so much unrest in a single year of your life that you matured a decade or two beyond your time? Enter the world of head injury. I had just turned twenty-six when I was introduced to a level of stress and responsibility that shouldn't be part of anyone's life. I am as much of a survivor as my former common-law partner—and he's the one who sustained the head injury!

John, my partner at the time, had taken a work transfer that moved him from Canada to the U.S. I accompanied him as a visitor, so I could not work or volunteer. For a few weeks, I was carefree, but I soon became restless, and began to feel as though I was losing my identity. I tried not to show it, though, because John loved his new job. He even purchased a motorcycle to celebrate.

Six days after he bought the bike, I received an early morning phone call. John had been in a motorcycle accident on his way to work, and had sustained a very severe brain injury, diagnosed as a diffuse axonal injury. He was in a coma, and had to be airlifted to the nearest medical center that could manage his condition, two hours away from where we were living.

I spent the next three weeks in the hospital. John's parents flew out for support. His coworkers stopped by periodically and assisted me as best as they could, even though they hardly knew me. My own family and friends did their best to support me on a long-distance basis, and we even received financial donations from John's union and our personal network to help cover food and bills. Despite it all, I was mostly alone in dealing with the medical teams and our personal affairs, and in coping with my own emotions.

After those first three weeks, our insurance company determined that John's medical bills were too high to keep him in the U.S., so we had to move back to Canada. The stress, sadness, and fear I felt in those weeks were overwhelming at times. I lost weight, and would frequently cry uncontrollably in my hospital residence. My entire life was being uprooted, but in the face of John's need, my well-being was not a priority.

When he was stable enough to be removed from a respirator, John and I were airlifted to Alberta, Canada. He spent another three months in the hospital, and so did I. This is where I really began to learn about brain injury and how much it affects not only the injured person, but everyone involved in his or her life.

Eventually, John was discharged, but he was far from independent. For the first few weeks, he needed to be monitored at all times, and he wasn't safe alone. He had problems with his balance and coordination, blurred vision, severe short-term memory issues, difficulty with word finding, and trouble concentrating. More, he was impulsive, and had trouble with initiation, judgment, managing his mood, and many other cognitive functions. For me, it was like dealing with a three-year-old. My patience was pushed to its limits, but I was determined to make sure he recovered.

At this point, I still had no concept of what level of control I had over this situation. I was a full-time caregiver putting 110% of my energy into John's well being. I challenged him daily to ensure he was making progress.

Within two months, John was well enough that I could leave him at home alone, and find employment. Three months after that, John was able to go back to work in his pre-injury field. This did not mean he had fully recovered: the damage to his vision was permanent, and he was still learning to compensate. His driver's license had been revoked, so he either used public transit or relied on me to act as his chauffeur. He continued to have difficulty with his short-term memory, executive functioning, and word finding, and we started to realize that many of his long-term memories had been lost as well. Much of our history together, he no longer remembered. It was so disappointing. I felt like all the effort I'd put into our relationship prior to his accident had been for naught.

The highly social side of his personality, part of what had originally attracted me to him, was not coming back. He still had difficulty with initiation, so I became both secretary and mother, helping him with planning and providing regular prompts to ensure he followed through with his personal commitments and his responsibilities at home. He still had difficulty with impulsivity, and made reckless purchases. Where before his behavior had been that of a toddler, now it was like dealing with a teenager. I could only say so much, though, because he was more sensitive now and could get extremely angry. Sometimes, when we'd argue, he would storm out of the house, threatening never to come back. It took all I had to not run after him, but I had to let him go in order for both of us to learn from this behavior. I would be raging mad at him, and at the same time scared to death of what he might do while he was gone. During these absences, I couldn't focus on anything, and whatever I had been doing was put on hold. He always came back safely, but that didn't make it any easier.

Even when we weren't fighting, I worried about him. He had a dangerous job, and he was still vulnerable due to his visual deficit, reduced speed of information processing, and sporadic poor judgment. Complex physical tasks could be challenging, because he still struggled with coordination. I felt he was vulnerable in social settings as well. I would get so scared for him. I made a lot of check-up phone calls.

John continued to recover over the next two years—but our relationship, unfortunately, did not. Only some aspects of John's pre-injury personality returned. He was a good person, and I cared about him deeply, but I missed the old John—the John I'd fallen in love with. After so long in a caregiver role, I found myself struggling to let it go. Finally, we had an honest discussion. We recognized that our relationship had reached a point where we were so focused on what wasn't working that we couldn't put any energy into improving our quality of life. The only way either of us could feel normal again was to be apart. He was tired of my mothering, and needed to rediscover his independence; I needed to be with someone I didn't need feel the need to monitor or protect. More than anything, we each wanted the other to be happy, and move forward.

John and I separated after five and one-half years together—nearly three of them post-brain injury. Despite all the stress I endured and energy I expended, I would not take back this experience, which was thoroughly laced with valuable life lessons. Life is too short for unnecessary discouragement and judgment, especially when you are vulnerable. I have grown to recognize the people in my life who support me, and restrict time with those who do not serve a positive purpose. I believe this lesson started with John, and I will be forever thankful to him for helping me learn it.

I have also learned how easy it can be to lose yourself in someone else's problems. John needed me, and I was there, but at great personal expense. In trying to help him recover his life, I lost much of my connection to myself. Slowly, with the help of friends, family, and a support group for caregivers, I was able to schedule some "me time" and gain a sense of who I was, and what I wanted from my life—but it was hard to ask for that help. At first, I thought that by reaching out for aid I'd be labeled as weak or damaged (which was, incidentally, how I'd formerly viewed the attendees of support groups), but upon meeting others who not only understood but commended me for my efforts, I was able to ditch my insecurities.

It was from this experience that my personal motto was born: "Maintain your identity to keep your sanity!"

Juicy Questions

Does this story speak to you? The journaling prompts below can help you access messages from your authentic core, and integrate the richness and insights of this story into your own juicy, joyful life!

Have you ever played a major role in someone else's crisis or transition?

_____

_____

_____

_____

Are you, or have you been, in a situation where your own needs are subsumed by the needs of someone you love or are caring for? How has this affected your emotions, personality, and behavior?

_____

_____

_____

_____

Crystal was reticent about joining a support group, but it became a great resource for her. How do you feel about asking for help?

_____

_____

_____

_____

The Door to Miracles

Kate Michels

"Somewhere over the rainbow...Where troubles melt like lemon drops, that's where you'll find me..." – *E.Y. Harburg*

"Miracles happen every day." When people call me, that's the message they hear on my voice mail.

When I talk to them after, they often say, "Sure, miracles are happening every day—somewhere, for someone else. But how can I get a miracle to come my way?"

"Miracles happen for everyone," I reply. "I say this with certainty, because I know it is true. I know what miracles are, and I know how they happen. Maybe you've already had a miracle in your life, and you just didn't see it."

It is easy for me to ask for miracles, to see them and receive them, because I know my value and the value of every other human being. When my clients call me and ask, "Will you help me manifest this miracle?" I ask, "Are you sure you're ready?"

People often think they want something very badly; they ask for it, pray for it, mull over it. But then, when it shows up, they do not even recognize it, because it is better, brighter, different, and often far bigger than what they thought they were asking for.

Miracles are usually not the rainbows; they are found in the hearts of storms. They show up like tornadoes, whirlwinds in our lives. But in these stormy times, we find out who we really are. We find out if we can keep our word to ourselves and our higher power. We discover if we can remain grateful even as our house blows down around us. We discover that if we reach deep within ourselves to find our inner strength, and recognize our true value, we can do whatever it takes to follow through.

A new life shows up after cancer. A new career emerges after you get fired. Financial freedom marches in after the stock market fails. This is not a silver-lining concept; it is an acknowledgment that you have the ability to create and accept what you really want. Dorothy went looking for "somewhere over the rainbow," but the power to come home was within her the whole time. Miracles come to us *for* us, and because of us.

Every day, I stand tall in my knowledge of miracles so that every person can know their truth, walk out from behind their personal shadow, and let go of their doubts. I have had my share of storms in my life; many times, it seemed like it was all too much to bear. I, too, looked for that "somewhere over the rainbow," that place where I could leave my fears behind. Lost, far from home, scared and confused, I would say to myself, "This is a good time for a miracle." But then, I would realize that my miracle had already happened. The tornadoes that blew my house down provided me an opportunity to rebuild my life in a new, more beautiful, more miraculous way.

At eighteen years old, just out of high school and starting my first year at a good college, I was living in beautiful Santa Barbara, California when I found out I was pregnant. This was my first tornado, a whirlwind that picked me up and carried me far from what I'd planned for my life. I found myself in the strange new land of motherhood, suddenly catapulted from childhood to adulthood, spinning with fear and uncertainty, asking, "Am I strong enough to handle this?"

Then, I didn't know that the values, knowledge, and courage to overcome all obstacles already dwell inside each of us. If not for that magnificent storm, I might not know it so well today. When I began my journey, I didn't know what I wanted from my life, or even who I really was, but if I hadn't undertaken it, I might never have experienced all the other miracles that this first miracle brought my way.

The next storm hit twenty-nine weeks later, when my baby was born two and a half months early. The doctor proclaimed, "She is too small to live. It will be a miracle if she survives." As it turned out, my daughter was the smallest baby ever to survive at that hospital at that time. Twenty-nine years later, my daughter has a beautiful miracle baby of her own—my grandson.

The pregnancy I had not planned was a miracle in my life that taught me more about who I am, and what I am on this earth to do, than I could possibly have learned at college. My perspective shifted, my direction changed, and my life realigned in miraculous ways. Our home not only became a home for me and my baby, but for other unwed mothers who didn't know who they were, or what they should do. Lost and confused, looking for direction and support, they often found their way to my front door. Later, I opened my door to the children whose mothers and fathers couldn't deal with the trouble and tornadoes that life brings. These children, to me, were miracles waiting to be reclaimed.

Then, I opened prison doors, to share the miracle of acceptance with young men who had created their own tornados. Other doors opened to support abused women, men who abused themselves with drugs, businesspeople who were losing everything, and people whose life storms had been so devastating that they'd lost the will to live. Now, I use the telephone as a door into the hearts of people around the globe, opening myself on a daily basis to those who need to know the miracle that they are, and share the difference they can and do make in the world.

When I was eighteen, I asked for a miracle: that I could grow up to be a person who would really make a difference. I thought that a college diploma with "Dr. Kathryn" written on it was what I needed, but what I received from life was so much more. I asked to change the world, but a miracle showed up and changed *my* world. The tornado that carried me so far from what I had planned was the miracle that made the difference in me. I am a walking, talking, living miracle—and so are you!

Many more miracles appeared in my life after the birth of my daughter: my depression at twenty, the illness that almost took my life when I was twenty-three, my car accident when I was thirty-nine, my divorce. There was the experience of meeting my new husband, and the house we built together; the cancer that affected both my daughters; the real estate crash of 2008. Even the most traumatic accidents and events were all for the good, because they stirred up thoughts, beliefs, and feelings that impacted the way I live, and helped me to serve others. Behind every storm is a rainbow waiting to be seen.

Now, with the birth of my grandson, I have once again been carried off to an unknown place filled with miracles waiting to happen. I'm not sure where I will land—but I know it will be somewhere over the rainbow!

Juicy Questions

Does this story speak to you? The journaling prompts below can help you access messages from your authentic core, and integrate the richness and insights of this story into your own juicy, joyful life!

What does the word "miracle" mean to you?

_____

_____

_____

_____

Kate believes that miracles are present in life's challenges. When have you found a miracle in the face of adversity?

_____

_____

_____

_____

When a miracle appears, you have to be ready to receive it. What miracles do you pray for? What elements of these miracles are already present in your life?

_____

_____

_____

_____

GO FOR IT!
Chasing
YOUR *Dreams*

Live Boldly

Sue Landis

Living boldly is not about taking unmeasured risks; it's about reclaiming who you are in the pursuit of your dreams. Dreams are, in so many ways, your heart speaking to you. Listen to this inner voice, because somewhere in its calling lies a truth you may not yet have seen.

I have always felt compelled to set courageous goals. My journey has taken me from New Zealand sheep farmer's daughter to global leader in the London head office of a multi-national corporation. I owned the lease on a pub in England, built a successful real estate brokerage in the U.S., and became the inspirational force behind an international coaching business.

Living life to the fullest has also meant living within the boundaries of my awareness levels at any given time. While this has not always resulted in sweetness and roses, and has produced some rather unexpected side effects, I have learned to relish these experiences as gifts of learning which have led me to richer, more joyful places.

For example, the primary side effect of focusing intently on my corporate career was that I made relationship choices which were not a good fit. By the time I got to England, I was earning a generous six-figure income, but my personal life was falling apart. In the process of establishing my brilliant career, I had completely neglected to learn the art of personal happiness.

Two ill-fitting relationships over a ten-year period left me feeling deeply disconnected from who I was as a person. After my second marriage broke up just eighteen months after I arrived in England, I began to make a conscious effort to unravel my personal choices, and discover why they had taken me further from the things I valued. During this time, I excelled at the brave face, and continued to turn up

185

at my London office each day as if nothing had happened, but at night I retreated into my own world to think things through. I also sought the help of a psychotherapist to gain perspective. If I was going to get my next personal relationship right, I knew I had to start with me.

While I passed these quiet evenings at home (in full avoidance of all men, I might add) my mind kept drifting over my goals for the future. For years, I had had a burning desire to compete internationally in a competitive sport, and although this dream seemed to have no logical place in my life, it kept popping up, and wouldn't go away.

It was hardly a convenient or practical time for me to become a competitive athlete. I was in my mid-thirties, enduring a daily one-hundred-mile round-trip commute to London, and was hardly in the best shape physically. No particular sport appeared to be a natural choice, and the odds seemed against me, but decided I had to take this dream seriously. My thoughts kept coming back to polo, that beautiful horseback sport. As a kid on the farm, I'd grown up riding bareback, but I hadn't been on a horse since I left home to follow my career to the big city. I was oblivious at the time as to why I derived so much joy from riding; I just knew that being in the saddle gave me a feeling of peace.

I chose polo over other horse sports because there was a polo field in my village. It was run by a couple with four daughters around my age, and I thought being there would give me the chance to make new friends and have a life outside of work. I promised myself I would be as frugal as possible until I was sure I was ready to commit to the sport. I hired ponies instead of purchasing them, and waited until my birthday before I bought myself a nice pair of leather riding boots.

One day, a friend with whom I'd shared my dream of competing internationally asked me if I knew about the Women's World Polo Championships, which were to be held in England in about a year. It was an "Ah-ha!" moment that captured my interest and imagination, and soon afterwards, my decision was sealed. I was going to compete in, and win, this event.

Over the ensuing three months my plan was hatched. I needed four polo ponies, a polo coach, a personal trainer, financing via sponsorship, a groom, a horse truck, a rented house with enough land and stables to keep the ponies... And of course, the most important thing: a world class team of professional female polo players. When I looked at my list, I was daunted: how I was going to put all of the pieces together, and pay for it? Yet, instead of stopping me in my tracks, the challenge became a grand adventure, and I was more determined than ever to pursue it. After all, this was as much about the journey as it was about winning that championship, because every step of this experience took me one step closer to reconnecting with the real me. I could feel myself getting fitter and healthier from the strenuous exercise, and I relished the opportunity to spend extended periods in the beautiful English countryside, sitting under a tree in the cool of the afternoon, discussing polo tactics.

After work each day, I would arrive at the polo field, where four fresh ponies would be saddled and waiting. I spent hours hitting the polo ball around the field with my coach, reviewing shots, strategies, and my riding technique over and over. I was working with an amazing team, and by the beginning of that spring, I had visited Argentina with my coach to buy my final two ponies. I had also obtained the corporate sponsorship I needed. Everything was falling into place.

187

By the time we rode out to the National Anthem on the day of the finals—yes, we made it to the finals!—I had already won that game a thousand times in my mind. The big match was played in record hot temperatures. By half-time, the score was almost tied, and our team talk was as intense and palpable as the mid-summer air. Even though protocol demanded that we leave decisions to the most experienced professional, I had such a strong feeling about what we needed to do to win that I took the reins, literally and figuratively, and shared my plan.

I wasn't hitting the ball well, so my strategy was to take the other team's best player—a French woman who was the number two female polo player in the world—out of the game by riding my pony alongside hers, sticking to her like glue so she couldn't hit the ball. I would use my strongest skill, my ability to ride, to give my teammates an opportunity to score goals.

It worked! When the final bell sounded at the end of the chukka (period of play) we had increased our lead significantly, and we held that lead for the rest of the match. The championship was ours! We were so proud on that podium, holding our trophy high.

While chasing the fabulous, impractical dream of winning the Women's World Polo Championships, some juicy and delightful spin-offs occurred. I started to mix in a world that had previously been beyond my imagination—a world of international polo players, celebrities, supermodels, sheikhs and Arabian princesses, English gentry, and even royalty. Polo opened up a world that was unreachable to most people. Perhaps the most outstanding experience was attending a ball at a polo club in Gloucestershire. My girlfriend, a world-class polo player, convinced me to attend the ball alone, promising that she would seat me at a table full of dashing single men. She wasn't kidding: it was terrifying and thrilling at the same time to look over the seating plan and see the names "William Wales" and "Harry Wales" next to mine! Needless to say, it was a deeply memorable night, and it just goes to show how making bold choices can give you gifts in the way of memories and experiences you never could have imagined.

The best moments of my polo experience, though, were the moments when no one was watching—when it was just me and my pony, out on the field, practicing shots in the early dusk. Hitting just one perfectly executed shot in an hour of practice was enough to make me burst with pride. To be at one with my pony at a full gallop was an absolute joy. While it was great to win that championship, the journey itself was the biggest gift, because it gave me back myself.

Subsequent to the process of finding the real me, I attracted my soul mate. That's how I ended up in the U.S. Unlike my previous relationships, this one fits me perfectly, because I know now who I am, and what I want and deserve from my life. When I'm older, I want to look back on my life with a tingling sense of accomplishment. I want to see abundant, joyful experiences peppered with the gifts of mistakes. I want to say to myself, "I can't believe I did that!"—and I never want to say, "I wish I had." This is my life: I owe it to myself to live boldly, and hold myself accountable to my dreams.

Juicy Questions

Does this story speak to you? The journaling prompts below can help you access messages from your authentic core, and integrate the richness and insights of this story into your own juicy, joyful life!

What is your biggest, most outlandish dream? What factors make you label it "outlandish?"

_____

_____

_____

_____

If money, time, and other factors weren't an issue, what steps would you take toward that dream? How would you make it work for you?

_____

_____

_____

_____

Sue says, "Dreams are your heart speaking to you." What do your dreams tell you about yourself, your aspirations, and your values?

_____

_____

_____

_____

Dare to Dream

Suzy Spivey

"Life is either a daring adventure or nothing at all."
– *Helen Keller*

M y life changed forever when I experienced my soul awakening on a cold, crisp day in 1995, in a remote Himalayan village. I was on a three week trek in the Mount Everest region of Nepal with a group of nine travelers, including the dear friend and colleague who had convinced me to join her on this adventure a mere month before. At the time, I knew very little about Nepal, and had never hiked more than a few hours at a time. I had never even been camping. As I considered taking this trip, my rational mind kept crying, "Are you crazy?"

But I do love an adventure, and the need to escape my current reality far outweighed the arguments of my rational mind. After years of working in corporate America, I was exhausted, and yearned for more meaning in my life. The idea of traveling halfway around the world to a remote, isolated region where no one could contact me was very appealing. I had spent the past thirteen years defining myself by a career I had fallen into just out of college, easily climbing the corporate ladder one rung at a time without much thought as to what I really wanted for my life. Progressing in a successful career simply seemed like the right thing to do at the time. Growing up in small-town Alabama, I was raised to be a people-pleaser, to "do the right thing." My life, thus far, had been lived in perfect accordance with the script I'd learned while growing up.

But a little voice inside was growing louder, imploring me to find the deeper purpose I was meant to serve—to do what I wanted, rather than what was expected of me. While I had no idea what my purpose was, I could no longer silence that voice.

That's how I found myself in the Himalayas.

The first week of the trek was exhilarating, but challenging. Constantly surrounded by our talkative group of nine, I found myself longing for space to reflect on what I was experiencing. It quickly became clear that this was far more than a sight-seeing trip for me.

When we reached 14,000 feet, with plans to trek even higher toward Mount Everest, I developed symptoms of altitude sickness, which worsened through the night. By morning, it was obvious that I would have to separate from the group, and descend several thousand feet to recover. As I watched the only people I knew in this faraway land disappear up the trail, I was gripped by fear. I had never felt so sick and alone in my life. My mind raced. What if my condition worsened, and I died here all alone? I couldn't even contact my family to let them know what was happening!

I stumbled down the trail with my guide, barely able to put one foot in front of the other, stopping every half-hour or so to vomit as the altitude sickness racked my body. The only thing that propelled me forward was the desperate need to collapse on a bed. My guide's Nepalese family generously agreed to take me in while the rest of my group continued trekking. No one in the family spoke English, and the only medicine they had to offer was hot garlic soup and kindness. Feeling extremely frightened and vulnerable, I gratefully accepted whatever they offered me.

I soon realized that words were not necessary to communicate with my hosts; their warm smiles and kind eyes communicated everything. As I began to recover, I was able to observe this family and their simple life in the village. They had very little in the way of material possessions, and none of the American standards for comfort like electricity and indoor plumbing. What they had was each other. They sat together around the fire, sharing meals, and telling stories. They sang and danced for entertainment. I marveled at the profound sense of happiness and joy they exuded.

During my stay, one of the villagers died after a prolonged illness, and I witnessed a Buddhist death ritual performed to ensure the safe passage of the soul. Priests and monks arrived to initiate the three-day vigil over the body. The village was transformed as the priests chanted, rang bells, beat drums, and called forth haunting sounds from their Tibetan long horns. The first night of the vigil, all of my senses were awakened by the exotic smells of incense, the glow of oil lamps, and those deep, resonant sounds. I watched through the night from my small wooden-shuddered window. It seemed to me that I was holding my own vigil for the death and reawakening of my own soul.

At dawn, as the sun crested the snow-covered peaks in the distance, I felt my soul awaken. No longer bound by expectations or the need to please anyone, I was able to just *be*. I felt more alive than I ever had before, and wept as feelings of peace, contentment, and joy flooded my heart.

Surrounded by the majesty of the Himalayas, I experienced a new sense of self. Dwarfed by the beauty all around me, I witnessed myself as a tiny speck on the earth. From that perspective, I was able to see my worries, fears, and doubts in a whole new light. If I were just a tiny speck, how could my fears—of failure, not being accepted, not doing the "right" thing—even exist? With this new awareness, my fears simply dissolved, and with their dissolution I felt connected to everything. I became part of the world in a way that I had never experienced before.

This awakening solidified my commitment to uncover my true purpose and seek more meaning from my life. I began to follow the wisdom of my inner voice, and established a daily practice of expressing gratitude. I studied with teachers who inspired me and helped me develop the necessary skills to believe in myself and my dreams. I redesigned my life on my terms, and held true even when people in my life didn't understand my choices. I chose to pursue my passions as a necessary step in finding my own true path; for example, I trained to lead people in creative expression through dance, which in turn reconnected me to the sense of joy and freedom I'd experienced in Nepal. I also trained to become a life coach, and at last realized my life purpose: to help others find their own true path by breaking through obstacles and self-limiting beliefs.

"The Journey of Life," became my theme, and "Daring to Dream" my motto as I journeyed around the world and within. Along the way, I pursued my goals of helping others, working with Habitat for Humanity to restore a village in Thailand hit by the tsunami. Continuing my self-exploration, I've completed advanced trainings in coaching, learning specific techniques to uncover one's true purpose, which deepened my desire to help others do the same. I continually seek new experiences to deepen my spiritual understanding, most recently with a month-long trip to initiate my second half of life in Bali.

My greatest lesson has been that when I say yes to life—when I take action on the opportunities that land in my path, even when they seem improbable or impossible—events unfold in a magical way. One example is how I came to host and produce my TV show, "Daring to Dream."

My life flows like a river, at times bubbling over with joy, at times taking unexpected turns, and occasionally encountering rocks that momentarily block the flow. I allow them to serve as reminders to let go and allow the current to take me downstream in the direction of my purpose—helping others dare to dream.

Juicy Questions

Does this story speak to you? The journaling prompts below can help you access messages from your authentic core, and integrate the richness and insights of this story into your own juicy, joyful life!

Are you living according to your dreams, or following a "script" given to you in your early life?

_____

_____

_____

_____

Think of a time when you were completely out of your element, as Suzy was in that Himalayan village. How did it change your perspective?

_____

_____

_____

If you were to view your life from a great height, what would it look like? By seeing your fears as smaller and less encompassing, how can you gain a new appreciation for your potential?

_____

_____

_____

_____

Climb Every Mountain

Simran Singh

When I look back on my life, I see it through the kaleidoscope of the experiences I've lived through; fragments swirl, creating a beautiful picture of light and dark. I grew up walking a fine line between two cultures, always searching for where I fit in. I knew I was different—or at least, I thought I was. That is the illusion, isn't it? We all believe we are so very different.

I have discovered that looks, mannerisms, gifts, and experiences may be unique, but we all have three things in common. First, every individual desires to experience deep love. Second, every person feels isolation and pain. And third, it is our experience of pain, chaos and dysfunction which ignite our inherent greatness. However, the expression of that greatness requires a willingness to say yes to both the love and the pain.

I spent thirty years in fashion retail, beginning at age four, when I started helping out in the family business. My parents were first-generation immigrants who had arrived in the U.S. with only eight dollars, and they worked hard. I learned that love meant working. The harder I worked, the greater the connection I felt with them.

Thirty years passed in a series of unmemorable moments. Life was about completing a task and moving to the next one with no acknowledgement, and no rest. I became a multitasking machine, a human *Do*ing rather than a human *Be*ing.

Although I loved the fashion business and was successful in it, over the years it began to feel repetitive. I became increasingly unconscious, going through the motions, not really present for any of it. I had difficulty remembering what happened over the course of the day, and who came into the store. I would leave work only to go home and work some more. I lost my feelings, and I lost myself. I was deadening.

Because I could not value myself enough to take care of *me*, I lost two children in miscarriages. My husband left. I could no longer look in the mirror, because all I could see was a dying spirit, a woman I did not recognize. I realized that if I went back to the family business, I would die. My body was physically illustrating this fact. In order to live, I had to walk away from everything I knew myself to be.

I sank into a deep depression. By working hard and doing what I thought was right, I had lost everything that held meaning. I was utterly alone.

Except for the numbers.

Throughout my whole life, the number 11 would mysteriously appear whenever I needed answers or confirmation. I saw it on clocks, license plates, receipts, buildings, and cabs. It became the language of my dialogue with the Universe.

As I sank deeper into darkness, I slept a lot. When I awakened, the clock always read 1:11 or 11:11. If I ventured to the kitchen, the microwave flashed 11:11, regardless of what time it actually was. Three weeks and dozens of 11:11 appearances later, I'd had enough. "What do you want with the 11s?" I asked angrily. "Tell me, or stop!"

In that moment, I received a download. It was a magazine, complete from cover to cover. I experienced the logo, style, dimensions, what the paper felt and smelled like. I saw the colorful graphics, and the name, *11:11 Magazine—Devoted to the Journey of the Soul.*

In my own head and in my own voice, something spoke the words, "Do this *now!*"

The Universe knew I was a workaholic, so a project was the perfect thing to get me out of bed. I had no experience in the magazine industry, but I dutifully sat down at the computer and started typing. I contacted feature interviews; they all said yes. In thirty days, I had completed the premier issue.

Then, fear began to mount. I knew nothing about graphics. "God," I said, "If you want *11:11 Magazine* to happen, you have to bring me a graphic designer."

That night my computer crashed. I was sure everything I'd done was lost, but after many stressful hours the serviceman finally retrieved the material. He asked what I was working on, and I told him I was creating a life enhancement magazine. His reply: "I don't know if you need help, but my friend is a fabulous graphic designer."

It was the sign I'd prayed for. *11:11 Magazine* was going to be real!

While the process excited me, I was also gripped by fear. This project was a mountain, a behemoth! To get past my fears, I decided to climb a real mountain—Mount Kilimanjaro.

I did everything necessary to promote and complete *11:11*, without holding back. If I became afraid, I looked at a picture of Kili and say, "The magazine is not a mountain, but Kili is!"

The day after final proofing, I arrived in Africa, and—along with porters, two guides, and a cook—began the 19,500-foot trek. With every inch came insight, gratitude, courage, and lessons for living. In total, there were seven lessons, and I carry them with me still.

The journey began with the guides saying "Polay, polay," which means, "Slowly, slowly," almost constantly. First lesson: walk slowly, and breathe in everything. Take my time. I have only this moment.

The climb was mentally and physically challenging. I had not trained the way I'd intended, and I had not put on additional weight as the guide books suggested. Second lesson: often, I do everything but what I most need. I let other things become more important than time for myself.

The hike was solitary, but each hut station was a frenzy of people from all over the world. Third lesson: We are all the same, wanting to share our joys, sorrows, and dreams, waiting to discover our depths and our heights.

As I ventured higher, the temperature cooled, but the porters, wearing light clothing and flip flops, ran the whole route with fifty-pound bags upon their heads. They smiled exuberantly, waving and shouting, "Jambo!"—"Hello," in Swahili. Fourth lesson: It is easy to carry the weight of the world on my shoulders with a smile. It simply requires that I choose to do so.

The air got thinner, and I moved more slowly. One guide stayed with me. We arrived at Kibo hut, the last stop before the summit, an hour after the rest of our group. Fifth lesson: It does not matter at what

199

speed I travel; we will all reach the same place. I am exactly where I am supposed to be.

The summit was the steepest part of the climb, and temperatures plummeted below zero degrees. Some people chatted excitedly about reaching the top, while others were concerned about altitude sickness and edema. Midnight arrived, and we began the upward climb. The air was so thin that each step was exhausting. Cries of "Polay, Polay!" echoed in the night air. The path wound snakelike, maneuvering around scree and snow. I found myself lightheaded and out of breath. I would walk a few steps and pause, walk a few more steps, then pause again. Sometimes I would get sick when I stopped, but my guide would coerce me to continue, saying, "Let's go."

A mere thirty minutes from the summit, my head started spinning. Why, I wondered, did I allow myself to remain in situations that make me feel bad, rather than changing direction in order to feel good? Sixth lesson: I victimize myself when I don't listen to my body.

Once I learned that, I realized that I'd gotten what I came for.

The experience was not about reaching the summit; it was about the journey. Each step I took up that mountain signified a step I'd taken in my life; a step for each breath, each word, each page, each hesitation, each tear shed. On this journey, I was able to bring myself back to my life, step by step. The hike was symbolic of life itself: move slowly, breathe, step, breathe, keep moving, breathe, keep climbing, breathe…Then, stop. Rest. Acknowledge the victory. Celebrate the person I am, the person I was, and the person I will be.

I returned to Kibo hut feeling complete. Soon, the other hikers returned. Some were upset because they did not summit. Others gloated about reaching the top, and were already ready for another endeavor. Seventh lesson: When I fixate on the result, the goal, or the accomplishment, I miss out on the joy of the experience. The journey is as much in the peaks as in the valleys.

I spent the next two days on safari in Lake Manyara and Ngoro Ngoro Crater. I returned to neatly stacked cases of *11:11 Magazine's* premiere issue.

Three months later, *11:11* had subscribers all over North America. Six months after that, *11:11* was in a national retail chain. One year later, *11:11* added talk radio, which quickly became syndicated.

I know now that there is no mountain I cannot climb. When we get out of the way and allow the Universe to work in and through us, magic happens. Who I have become is who we all are, if we only believe, and step beyond the illusion.

Juicy Questions

Does this story speak to you? The journaling prompts below can help you access messages from your authentic core, and integrate the richness and insights of this story into your own juicy, joyful life!

Often, the tasks we assign ourselves, or which the Universe assigns to us, seem insurmountable. What is your "Mount Kilimanjaro?" How can you come to terms with your own mountain?

_____

_____

_____

_____

Do you give yourself time to stop and breathe? Or do you try to plow through every task without rest?

_____

_____

_____

_____

Do you tend to focus more on your destination than on your journey? What can you do to slow down—to "Polay, polay"—and appreciate each step as a miracle?

_____

_____

_____

_____

What Are You Thinking?

Judy Aleman

There are moments in life which can shape or change who we are and how we live. Sometimes, they're important events—marriage, divorce, birth, or death. Other times, they can seem like minor occurrences; little things that catch your attention as you go about your day, conversations which shift a thought process.

I experienced one of those "minor" moments one quiet summer evening in New Orleans, when my mother came home from a meeting and enthusiastically announced to the family, "I am becoming a new person!" She said that, by simply choosing different thoughts, she could change her life.

This was a totally new concept to our family. Growing up in a very traditional household, I was taught that life should follow a predictable path, unfolding much as it had for my parents and their parents. I would live close to home, get a decent job, marry, and have children. Being able to impact the direction of my life simply by thinking new thoughts seemed radical, yet I instinctively knew that there was something special about what energized my mother that evening.

What I didn't realize was how significantly that conversation would impact my life.

I am a quiet and shy person by nature—so shy that my family nicknamed me "the shadow," because I would hide to prevent anyone from looking at me. Over the years, I've learned not to dwell on these limiting traits; instead, I've trained myself to shift the thoughts which flow through my mind day in and day out, allow them to become more constructive and expansive.

In many ways, I owe this practice to my mother. Although she soon forgot her declaration and went about her life as she always had, her words stuck with me. I came to understand how something as natural and simple as guiding my thoughts through life's ups and downs can make a huge difference in how my life unfolds. Rather than allow my timid nature to take over and isolate me, I take a deep breath, summon courage from within, and take on life with curiosity and openness. When I shift my thoughts from self-doubt to curiosity, life gets a whole lot more fun and interesting. Day-to-day life has enough bumps and challenges; the last thing I need to do is add to them by cultivating my unwarranted fears, worries, and doubts!

Instead of remaining in New Orleans like my childhood friends, I found a job that would expand my experience of life. I became a flight attendant for a major carrier and travelled the world. Seeing how people in other cultures live helped me better understand human nature, and how lives unfold.

After a few years of flying, though, I became restless, and looked for other positions within the company. A part of me was afraid to make the move—until I remembered my mother's words, and shifted my thoughts away from my fear of change. I accepted the challenge, and this new phase of my career enabled me to learn new skills as it expanded my confidence and expertise.

As life progressed, I found satisfaction and value professionally and personally. I married, raised my two children, and found ways to juggle all of the responsibilities that life presented. If you looked at my life from the outside, it would have seemed organized, fulfilling, and successful. I had a satisfying career with a company that supported my wanderlust, an affluent lifestyle, an active family life, and a supportive circle of friends. But while on many levels my life did seem ideal, in my quiet moments, I knew intuitively that the work I was doing wasn't what I was meant to do. There was an unsettling restlessness, a feeling that something was missing—but I didn't know what.

After a lot of soul searching, I decided to leave the corporate world. I sensed that I'd never discover "what's next" if I continued doing what I was doing. After working for the same company for my entire adult life, leaving took a giant leap of faith. To make things more challenging, my marriage of twenty-three years dissolved, and I had to deal with the loss of the family structure that meant so much to me. To say that my world was turned upside down is an understatement. I doubted my worth. I felt abandoned. When I looked in the mirror, I saw a pudgy, middle-aged, unemployed woman who was sure she would never find love again. My life had lost its purpose, and I was unprepared for the decisions that lay before me. I wallowed in self-pity and inertia, feeling like a failure.

Then, I remembered that conversation with my mother. How had I forgotten it, and gotten so off track? I realized that I had let my positive, resilient attitude slip away, and fallen victim to the destructive cycle of unhealthy thoughts. Telling myself I was "too busy" to maintain the healthy habits that had once been a cornerstone of my life, I had lost my focus, and let the day-to-day issues cloud my greater vision for how I wanted to experience my life.

That was a turning point for me. Then and there, I made a conscious decision to reclaim my life. I vowed to pay more attention to my thoughts and choices, knowing that they were powerful allies in my quest to become happier and healthier. By aligning my thoughts with my values and goals, I was able to create a powerful force, a "superhighway" that simplified my decision-making process, and helped me identify what was truly important so I could move forward in a constructive and responsive way.

By paying attention to what was important to me, I was able to slim down, rebuild my resilient attitude, and create a rewarding new career. Today, using my talent and life experiences, I work to help women who are successful on the outside create more success and happiness in their personal lives.

My mother's words, spoken so many years ago, planted a seed within me that changed my life. So many people tell me that they wish they had a happier life, a better job, more leisure time, better health, or greater financial security—but that these goals seem to them to be beyond reach. Creating the life of your dreams isn't all about external activity: it takes a lot of internal work, as well. Like a garden, your creation will take planning. You'll need to gather the necessary tools, and work with patience and persistence, weeding out destructive

205

thoughts so that your bounty and potential can bloom. When you choose to think thoughts that support your values, aspirations, and priorities, your life will inevitably become more meaningful, juicy, and enjoyable.

So...What are you thinking about?

Juicy Questions

Does this story speak to you? The journaling prompts below can help you access messages from your authentic core, and integrate the richness and insights of this story into your own juicy, joyful life!

Do you know what you're thinking about? We think about 80,000 thoughts a day, most of which are the same thoughts we thought yesterday, and the day before. Pay attention to the things you think about most often. Are they are serving you well?

_____

_____

Often, life hands us situations over which, externally, we have little control. How can you change these situations in your life by doing some internal "gardening?"

_____

_____

_____

Judy was very shy as a child, but she didn't let this limit her. If you shifted your thinking around your own character traits, would your experience change?

_____

_____

_____

_____

The Dream Yet Discovered

Juanita Crawford Bobbitt

"There are only so many years between birth and death."

That was the comment with which my professor greeted me when I asked for his recommendation to accompany my application to a Master's degree program in economics. That remark, along with his disdainful facial expression, took me by surprise. I was approaching my fortieth birthday, and he was letting me know, in his view, that it was pointless, too late for me; I was already too old to consider a career as an economist.

I came of age in the late 1950s, when all society expected of a young girl was to be a good wife and mother. Still, I looked forward to attending college—although looking back, I'm not sure how much that goal was my idea, and how much was my mother's vision for me, as college was an opportunity my parents, both voracious readers, never enjoyed. Given my high-school grades, I was easily accepted at Brooklyn College. Upon earning my Bachelor's degree in Romance Languages, I began a graduate program in French, but soon left, eager to utilize the French and Spanish I'd learned in the "real world." I stumbled into a position at the United Nations at nearly the lowest grade. I saw this as a chance to polish my language skills.

I had been working for less than two years and was just beginning to learn what it meant to be an independent young adult when, one sunny Saturday morning, my dad asked me whether I had a few minutes to listen to a new album he'd bought. He'd taught me to appreciate music and I'd introduced him to jazz when I'd become acquainted with it at college.

"Later, Dad," I said, "I've got to go shopping." My girlfriend and I had planned a double-date at my home that evening, and I was preoccupied with entertaining. I took my kid brother with me.

When I called home to ask my mother a question, she said, "Your father's not feeling well." The tone of her voice told me immediately that something was wrong. We had to get home quickly.

I remember throwing my house keys to the floor, staring in disbelief at my father's body lying on the bathroom floor, his torso stretched out against the bathtub. A heart attack had taken him at just fifty-one years of age. We never got to share Thelonious Monk.

In the days that followed the tragedy, I decided I was responsible for my mother, whose life revolved around her husband and family, and for my fifteen-year old brother. It was a role I was totally unprepared for, given my sheltered existence.

The spiritual beliefs my parents had instilled in me, and support from family and friends, helped me through that painful, life-altering experience. But when I finally returned to work, my tight-knit family circle broken, I would suddenly find my heart racing. I didn't know anything about panic attacks. My doctor prescribed tranquilizers and I wouldn't leave home without them, but after some months, I grew concerned that I would become addicted to them. I found the courage to flush them down the toilet. To my surprise, it was easy, and I never looked back.

As I grew older, I sometimes wondered how my life might have been different had my father lived to a ripe old age, but over time, I've learned that life occurs in the present moment—what happened yesterday, last year, when I was a kid…It's all over. Good or bad, I can't change any of it. It's not what happened, but rather the story I hold onto about the experience that can limit me. I keep the good memories close, allow a few moments each day to connect to the Divine and my own inner core and purpose, and keep moving forward.

I continued to apply myself diligently to each UN assignment, and by the time I reached my mid-thirties, I found myself working in an area I loved: economic and social development. I had the honor of knowing many women from around the world who had, with little economic or other means of support, accomplished great things for their communities and themselves. They taught me that it's not always what you have; it's what you believe in. Nonetheless, I saw the importance of a solid grounding in economics to my chosen field. I grew to understand the role it played in the distribution and consumption of resources worldwide.

Studying economic theory seemed daunting, but I tested the waters, signing up for my first macroeconomic course. Receiving an "A" emboldened me, and I decided to take the plunge and apply to graduate school.

And then, my professor told me I was wasting my time.

I have learned that it's what you do when you are frightened or unsure that brings the greatest reward. I refused to listen to my naysayer. I was clear about my goals, so I chose to use his doubts to clarify my objectives and strengthen my resolve. If I failed, I would consider it a lesson, not a breakdown. If I gave up without even trying, however, I would never achieve my goal.

In the face of his doubt, I insisted, explaining my motivation. As I'd achieved an "A" in his course, he was hard pressed to deny me the letter. After five years of night school, one course at a time, I received my Master's degree in Economics.

211

Thanks to a departmental reorganization, I had a new supervisor who saw promise in me and suggested I apply to the Kennedy School of Government at Harvard University. I headed off to Cambridge, Massachusetts, divorced and with a fourteen-year-old son, for the most rewarding academic experience of my life. It took strong desire and a willingness to plan, as my acceptance came without money. I had to convince my advisor to allow me to postpone entrance for a year while I got my finances in order. I also wanted my son to graduate elementary school before I moved him to a new environment.

After Harvard, I returned to the UN and traveled extensively on a number of worldwide assignments in public administration and women in development. In my spare time, I undertook volunteer activities and community service projects aimed at supporting women to realize their full potential. I am grateful for the ways in which I've been able to use my talents to make a difference for others.

After nearly forty years of service, I retired, having reached a senior professional level. Many might assume that it was now time to break out the rocking chair and the knitting, and buy a cat, but no—before retirement I'd organized a meeting in Switzerland for a group of women entrepreneurs, one of whom had suggested I look into obtaining a real estate license. "Hmm," I thought, "That would certainly be different from everything I've done to date!" Maybe, it was time to try something new. And so, while still consulting with the UN from time to time, I began a second career.

Ten years later, while still working as a broker, I recreated myself a third time—as a fiction writer. I am passionate about genealogy and exploring family history, and have always admired the pluck it took my grandmothers to travel alone at the turn of the last century from the small island of Barbados to the big city of New York to make it on their own. Over the years, I'd often thought about writing a fictional account, tracing a family's journey from the Caribbean and the Southern United States to New York City, but had held the thought on a back burner; "No time," I told myself. But, while I was sitting in a seminar, the leader asked our group, "What could you do in life that's so inspiring you could never grow tired of doing it?" I saw clearly that it was time to unleash my hidden passion for writing.

When I sit down to pore over genealogy and to write, I lose track of time. I am excited and lit up. It makes me know I am fulfilling and satisfying something deep within.

Reinventing oneself at every stage of life is rewarding; it means that you're continuing to learn, grow, and stay vital. It requires believing in oneself and having integrity in what you do. Age is not a factor. There are only so many years between birth and death, but I believe I've learned to make the most of them. I share my story to encourage every woman to live out her dreams; the old ones yet unrealized, and the new ones yet to be discovered.

Juicy Questions

Does this story speak to you? The journaling prompts below can help you access messages from your authentic core, and integrate the richness and insights of this story into your own juicy, joyful life!

Have you ever told yourself that you are too old, or too young, to pursue a dream?

_____

_____

_____

_____

Have you ever listened to a "naysayer," whose words or actions held you back from following your passion? How can you let those negative words go, and follow the direction of your heart?

_____

_____

_____

_____

If you could reinvent yourself in any career, what would it be?

_____

_____

_____

_____

A BUSINESS WITH
Passion AND
Purpose

Reborn...Again

Donna Cravotta

I am the third of four children, raised by a single mom who appointed me the caregiver for the family before I had a choice. A good portion of my childhood consisted of cooking, cleaning, and taking care of my siblings, even the older ones. I was often misunderstood, and felt as if I was looking in on my life from the outside, biding my time until my real life could begin.

When I started working, I met people of new dimensions. I thought, "These are my people." And they were, for a while.

Later, I started dating a more mature man. We traveled and lived what appeared to be a charmed life, surrounded by his friends and colleagues. I reinvented myself again and thought, "These are my people." And they were, for a while. But after several years, I'd had enough. It had been fun, but it was not *my* life.

Not long after that, I ran into a childhood friend, and we started dating. I literally baby-sat for him for seven years. I was terribly unhappy, but I stayed until I realized that this *couldn't* be my life. At age thirty-two, I escaped and finally began to come into my own.

I purchased my first home, an amazing co-op that I renovated on my own. I painted my living room walls purple, and painted clouds in my bathroom. I had a good job at a law firm. I traveled for business and pleasure. I took up distance bike riding. I wore a tiara, just because I could. For the first time in my life I, took care of *me*, and did whatever made me happy. It felt good, and there was no stopping me.

Then, forty began to loom in the not-too-distant future, and I caught a serious case of baby fever. I felt incomplete, and all the broken pieces of my own childhood came back to haunt me. I wanted my own child's experience to be whole. I also knew I would be an amazing mother: just as some people know that they should not have children, I knew that if I didn't it would be an enormous mistake.

I wanted a baby and I needed a mate, but I was working crazy law firm hours, so I decided internet dating was the way to go. In retrospect, this was not such a great idea. (Maybe my biological clock took over and clouded my judgment.) I did meet someone, and we are now co-parenting our amazing son—but my relationship with said co-parent (we'll call him Baby Daddy) has been one of the most difficult I've ever had, and has forced me to make challenging, sometimes life-altering decisions to protect my son's best interests.

Fast forward a few years from that meeting. My mom had been ill for a long time, and her illness reestablished many of our dysfunctional family lines. She lived in Florida, and I lived in New York, so I traveled back and forth, taking over my old role as family caregiver. In order to do this, I had to leave my precious four-year-old son alone with Baby Daddy, whom I did not trust. In a word, it sucked! But after my mom passed away, I was able to let go of some of the old harmful axioms that had defined my life. I was released.

So, I booted Baby Daddy out of my house. Then, I sold the house, purchased a condo, and bought bright purple curtains. I was still working crazy law firm hours, but now my bosses were allowing me to work from home (mostly so I could support the Asian and Abu Dubai offices at 3:00 a.m.). I experienced daily "Calgon moments," and was increasingly terrified of the prospect of Baby Daddy—who was consumed by irrational fears but in total denial of his mental illness—becoming the primary parent in our little family. It was clear that my balancing act was not going to work out in the long term, so I started looking for a better way.

I discovered the virtual assistance industry while poking around on the internet. "Whammo!" I thought. "This is it! I can do this. I *am* doing this!" I agonized over a business name, then incorporated, built a really bad web site, and sketched out a business plan. Then, I sat back and thought, "Now what?" I was still working a million hours per week, so I developed Plan A: scale back at work, and take a year to build my business, which would target sole practitioner lawyers and real estate professionals.

Plan B: Two weeks later, while I was eating ice cream for dinner at 9:00 p.m., the man behind the counter asked if I was okay. I smiled an enormous, toothy grin, and said, "I'm quitting my job tomorrow!"

This was completely out of character for me. I'd been at the firm for seventeen years, and, given my childhood experiences, longevity and financial security were very important to me. (Since then, I've learned that my "secure" job was loaded with false security, and although it was a great risk to walk away, in the long run owning my own business will offer me much more security, longevity and happiness than any law firm could. Still, it was hard to let go.)

My boss freaked out, and hired me as a consultant to finish up a few key projects. At first this was a good thing, since I needed the money—but I soon hated every minute. These people were holding up my progress! I got to the point where I was taking conference calls in my car in the dead of winter, because I didn't want the law firm in my house or in my life. These were not my people anymore. I had already moved on.

All the while, my self-talk was screaming, "How are you going to pull this off? Who's going to hire you? Are you insane?" These statements were reiterated by my family and several friends. I just tuned them out and forged ahead.

The first thing I learned was that most of the experience I had accumulated over twenty years of working in corporate law firms meant absolutely nothing in the real world. Toward the end of my law firm career, my major tasks seemed to be putting out fires and sitting in on fruitless meetings. There was so much waste. But when you're a solo entrepreneur or a small business owner, you're accountable for everything. I had to learn to work without support teams, and on a tiny budget. I had to research applications and processes that make small businesses efficient, then learn how to market myself. I refused to take on clients until I could comfortably do the work, and my savings account took a big hit.

Since I started my business, my plan has changed several times. My clients are neither lawyers nor real estate professionals. My only "niche" is that I take work that I like, and work with people I like.

219

I get a charge when my clients get that first glimmer of how I can help them. It gives me great joy to look at my calendar and see business engagements side-by-side with my son's birthday parties, activities and play dates. I am fully immersed in my business and my son's life; they are equally important, and it's documented. This *is* my juicy, joyful life!

I have been in business since 2006, and both my business and I continue to grow and change. I have learned to trust my inner voice: we are now friends. One of the highlights of owning your life professionally and personally is that if something does not work in the morning, you can implement a new plan by the afternoon. Intuition plays a big role in my business management.

Now that I am established, I can look back and see how all the pieces fit together, and how everything happened just as it was supposed to happen. I can clearly see how both good and bad experiences were necessary to bring me to the place I am today—a place where, for the first time, I feel that I belong. I live in a wonderful, supportive community full of work-from-home parents, and we have effectively created a village to raise our children. Here, I can build the life I want while being a strong role model for my son. I've found my people—but I haven't found all of them yet!

Juicy Questions

Does this story speak to you? The journaling prompts below can help you access messages from your authentic core, and integrate the richness and insights of this story into your own juicy, joyful life!

Do you ever feel as though you're living for someone else, or living someone else's life?

_____

_____

_____

_____

How can you make your life more authentically your own? Can you take ownership of what you want, and implement it in a positive way?

_____

_____

_____

_____

Does your work interfere with your family life? What changes can you make in order to be more present for your family? What sacrifices are you (and are you not) willing to make to create more balance between work and home?

_____

_____

_____

_____

Juice Your Own Lemonade

Tara Sage Steeves

As a Dream Realization coach, I know a thing or two about the beauty of dreaming, and about what it takes to make dreams come true—but this wasn't always the case.

I know what it means to feel stuck, overwhelmed, and constrained by circumstances. But even in the midst of my most trying times, I knew in my heart of hearts that, given the right tools, I could juice up a tall glass of lemonade from that pile of lemons I kept tripping on, and somehow create a life full of the sweet stuff—love, joy, freedom, abundance, and ease.

Lemons in tow, I set out to do just that.

Gazing dreamily out the window of my basement apartment, watching the sidewalk and the tires of passing cars, I ignored the persistent calls from creditors. I tried to smile at the sting of resurfacing childhood wounds, and work with the fact that I was living on as little as ten dollars a day. During this time, I was doing a series of odd jobs: bringing signs in and out for a flower shop down the street, flipping omelets at a nearby breakfast place. And through it all, I ached to be able to funnel my creative energy into something that excited me. I was ready to do whatever it took to create something better for myself—not because I was especially brave, but because I simply couldn't imagine that the journey could be any harder than staying put!

So I dug…deep. After voracious self-study and numerous trial-and-error experiments, I graduated from the prestigious Hard Knocks Academy with a heap of practical wisdom, and a bold and unwavering belief in possibility. I have more traditional credentials—the ones that make my mother proud, and rightly so—but most of my lessons came from living.

I resisted the pressure to get a 9-to-5 job, because I knew I wanted to start my own business. All that creative energy needed to go somewhere! However, financial stress (and those pesky creditors) finally led me to a research job that aligned with my Psychology degree. I took the job with an exit strategy in mind, and the clear intention that this long-awaited stable paycheck was nothing more than a vehicle to put food on my table and improve my credit standing.

About a year later, I moved out of my basement apartment into a two-family home. At that point, the banks were giving away mortgages like lollipops, and I considered my successful application a "planned coincidence." I had no clue how to fix a leaky faucet, or how to use a tool that wasn't a hammer or a paintbrush, but I managed to get the bigger of the two units rented. With my tenant's rent covering nearly the entire mortgage, I was paying less as a homeowner than I had been as a renter.

With my research job to pay the bills, I enrolled in a Coach Training program at night. Every morning, I was out of bed by 5:30, so I could study my notes and chip away at my business plan. I knew that it was only a matter of time before the research grant that paid my salary would end, and I wanted to be ready. When my boss finally sat me down and gave me the news that he had to lay me off, I practically skipped out of his office. My plan had taken enormous patience and persistence to pull off, but everything had come together beautifully. Not only had I reduced my living expenses by purchasing a home, I was able to collect unemployment while getting my new business off the ground.

At twenty-nine years young, I launched my coaching business. I was a regular at all the networking events. With my brand new business cards tucked into the pocket of one of the two businesslike outfits I owned, and my old car parked out of sight at least six blocks away, I burst onto the scene, and told anyone who would listen that "Life Coaching is what I do!"

I was soon to learn just how large a role this small business community would play in my entrepreneurial beginning.

While I was happy as an entrepreneur, business was far from booming. What I had hoped would feel fun and free was starting to feel a bit like running through cement. So, about a year after launching my business, I did what any poor, single, struggling entrepreneur would do: I took myself and my credit card on a ten-day vacation! Following intuition over logic, I flew to Nevada to meet up with friends, and we had a fun, savory, transformative adventure immersed in art and nature.

Refreshed, I was once again able to savor the heart-space I was in. But once I got home again, I found myself crying in parking lots simply because they were parking lots. I was suddenly claustrophobic in cars, and even in my own living room. I was acutely affected by the sadness of strangers passing by. "I no longer fit my life," I told my friends. "I've expanded, and I feel like I'm suffocating!"

Weeks passed, and these symptoms showed no sign of letting up. I was in desperate need of more room to explore and nurture my biggest, boldest dreams. Craving freedom, I'd all but decided to buy a one-way ticket anywhere, just to get out. "There just aren't enough places to dream here!" I professed. Either I had to create what I longed for, or travel the world looking for it. My friends, who had been trying to persuade me to stay put, reluctantly offered to help me pack.

But then, when I'd reached the end of my rope, something shifted. Over the next forty-eight hours (thankfully faster than I could pack), I found myself awake at the kitchen table in the middle of the night, scribbling down the ideas that were screaming in my brain. After patching them together, I decided to use my boldness, my outside-the-box thinking, my knack for "planned coincidences," and my coaching training to create an event like no other—an event now known as The Dream Party®. People would come to my event to celebrate the possibilities for their lives, sharing and exploring their dreams as if it were five years in the future and those dreams had already come true. They would, for a night, become who they dreamed they could be. As their "future selves," they could make connections and find guidance and support from others to help make their dreams real in the here and now.

225

While I was overjoyed to have received this inspiration (and more than a little relieved not to be moving house), I realized that the funds to support my middle-of-the-night download were not going to magically appear. It was totally intimidating, but I knew I had to figure out a way to bring my dream to fruition.

First, I needed a time machine.

The first "Help Wanted" ad I ever placed for my business read simply: "Time Machine Artist Needed." I was stunned when, within just two days, I received over forty responses from local artists eager to take the job. Step one: accomplished.

Step two: location, location, location. Regardless of my non-existent budget, I knew that this special event deserved special surroundings. With focused persistence, and no shortage of fear, I managed to negotiate my way into a stunning venue in Providence, Rhode Island for only $62 (the fee for a security guard). Relying on my wonderful networking community to spread the word, I started selling tickets to my "creative networking event."

While I suspected that other people might also need an inspiring, expansive space to dream, my initial motivation for The Dream Party® was based on my own needs. If there was ever proof that we're more alike than we are different, this was it. More than one hundred people showed up to my first event. Now, years later, The Dream Party® continues to touch the hearts of "closet creatives" and driven dreamers every day.

My experience has been that the sweet, juicy nectar of life awaits just beyond the prison of fear. Each step of the way, I continue to feel afraid, but that doesn't mean I am not brave. After all, if the brave felt no fear, what would they need bravery for? The difference is that I don't allow my fear to hold me back. I don't make excuses to let it rule my decisions, and I don't let it tell me my dreams are outlandish and impractical. In other words, I've stopped carting around my lemons, and started juicing my own lemonade!

My wish for you is that your dreams will always inspire more than they intimidate. Summon your boldest Self and forge ahead, knowing that the Universe rewards bravery. Your dreams will thank you.

Juicy Questions

Does this story speak to you? The journaling prompts below can help you access messages from your authentic core, and integrate the richness and insights of this story into your own juicy, joyful life!

Who do you want to be five years from now? What do you want to be doing with your life?

_____

_____

_____

_____

What fears hold you back from becoming that "future self?"

_____

_____

_____

_____

Look at your life as if you're looking at a stranger's life. If you were talking to a stranger who shared your dreams, what advice would you give them? What first steps would you tell them to take?

_____

_____

_____

_____

On Being Different

Lisa Reina-Frommer

"Metamorphosis: The caterpillar grows
Beauty unveils
Patterns unique emerge
No longer afraid."
–*Lisa Marie June*

S tanding tall at 5'3", my energy brightens the room. I am sitting behind an ornate wooden table. Relics, stones, crystals, mementos, and an Aleister Crowley Tarot deck lie upon a reading cloth of star-sprinkled purple velvet—a cloth made just for me and my special gift. Ego put aside, I am ready to help each and every person in need.

I was born with a gift of knowing.

As a young child, I was sweet, bossy, and overly protective of my younger siblings, but inwardly I felt uncomfortable and shy, because I knew I was different. I couldn't put my finger on what was so different about me, but I really felt it. I was never first in line, or the one who was always picked on someone's team. I became an outcast, and stuck to one friend at a time.

I was uncomfortable in crowds, and being in school drained me. I didn't understand that: wasn't it supposed to be fun to meet new people and go to new places? Instead, I was very self-conscious, and constantly aware of the energy around me. I turned into a people-pleaser because I couldn't stand the feeling of negative, angry energy. My parents argued a lot. My brother was always tormenting our little sister. I was molested by the family member whose attention and approval I most craved. I would sit on the front steps at night and glare at the looming moon, wondering if the happiness in life would ever outweigh the sadness.

229

I got through high school, and then went in through the back door in every profession that caught my interest. Rather than endure endless schooling, I challenged the state boards head on, and I always passed. I even learned physics with the help of a tutor to pass the ultrasound boards. Over the years, I had at least five different licensed careers, but none of them made me happy.

One magical day, a friend gave me a book on astrology and a copy of my natal chart, and told me to figure out how to read it. This complex and interesting subject was intoxicating to me: I couldn't get enough. I took classes—unusual for me—and purchased at least fifty books on astrology and other metaphysical subjects.

Learning about metaphysics brought to light something which, at that point, I hadn't yet shared with another soul. I just *knew* things: things that had happened, things that were going to happen. For example, I knew while I was still in high school that my parents would die before they were old. Every time they took a business trip I would cry all night before they left, and throughout the next day. At school, I would just sit at my desk and stare out the window, imagining every terrible thing that could happen. While they didn't die on a business trip, they did die young: my father passed away at age fifty-three of a heart condition, and my mother at sixty-two of pancreatic cancer.

I knew other things, too. One Sunday afternoon, as the sun shone bright and the flowers were blooming, my sister and I drove to the grocery store together. On the way home, I complained to her yet again about how mean my husband could be.

"How can you deal with him, Lisa?" she asked. "He is so controlling and intimidating!"

I had thought many times about leaving my husband for exactly those reasons, but in that moment, I *knew* I would not do so. I replied, "I am not going to have to deal with him for much longer, because he is going to die. I'm not sure when, or of what, but it won't be long."

My sister couldn't believe what I was saying. Yet less than a year later, my husband was diagnosed with leukemia. He passed away within ten months of the diagnosis, at the age of forty-four. Despite our problems, I was glad to be able to be with him in those last months.

When my husband left us, I was thirty-three years old. My children were just seven and three, and now they were dependent on only me. I set out to find out what was real in the metaphysical world, and what wasn't. I was still shaken that I had predicted my husband's death. Can you even imagine knowing such things about people, and not understanding why?

I visited Tarot readers, clairvoyants, and mediums, hoping to get some answers. Each time, they would end up giving me a deck of Tarot cards, and ask me to read for them instead! I couldn't believe this kept happening—but finally, I understood what I was meant to do.

I read first for my family, then for my friends, and finally for total strangers. People would break down and cry in front of me; each time that happened, I visualized soft pink light energy bathing them in love and compassion. My clients wanted to know how I knew so much about them, and often asked if someone had told me about them ahead of time. Of course I would never take information about anyone before a reading. I myself don't know how I know so much: I only know that I have a gift, pure and simple.

Here are two examples of what I've seen for people while reading their cards.

One long-time client, who will remain nameless, was working for a legendary musician, and was concerned about the longevity of his position. I told him this was the most stable long-term job of his career, and he needed to stick with it. Two weeks later, my client called me to say he'd been invited to an unusual private lunch with his boss, where he was asked, face to face, to stay with the organization for the rest of his life, on a perpetual contract.

Recently, I read for Heather, who works in a beautiful upscale salon. She was planning to attend two weddings, and asked if she would meet anyone special at these functions. "The first wedding will be delayed," I told her. "But you won't meet anyone at that wedding anyway. The second wedding, though, is out of town…Yes, you will meet a man who's a little older than you are. You will start a serious long-distance relationship!"

231

As it turned out, the first wedding was cancelled. At the second wedding, Heather met a great guy who's a little older than she is. They started a long-distance relationship, and now they're getting married.

There are an endless range of questions and topics that come to me through my astrology and Tarot readings. Everyone has questions, and they are all important. There are no questions that cannot be asked or answered.

Now, I no longer stare at the moon in gloom. Any tears that stream down my face are tears of gratitude. I am fifty-one years young, living a happy, juicy, joyful life. The Universe has given me a magnificent daughter, a brilliant son, and a new husband who's handsome, compassionate, and intelligent. My family is proud that I can use my gift to validate others and help them find their truth. I experience a miracle each and every time I sit at my beautiful table, and read for all the souls who need me.

"For the Sun and Moon are full of enlightenment
Our souls absorb them and become whole."

–Lisa Marie June

Juicy Questions

Does this story speak to you? The journaling prompts below can help you access messages from your authentic core, and integrate the richness and insights of this story into your own juicy, joyful life!

Have you ever felt that you were different than the people around you? How so?

_____

_____

_____

_____

How have your "differences" manifested as gifts in your life? How have they shaped who you are and what you do?

_____

_____

_____

_____

How can you use your unique talents to help those around you?

_____

_____

_____

_____

Create A Life You Love

Debbie Wysocki

On the day I watched my mother struggle to choose between purchasing medicine for my sister or buying food for our family, I knew I would never be poor. I would never depend on someone else to feed me, clothe me, or put a roof over my head.

Even as a child, I knew there had to be more to life than this constant struggle. I hated hearing that there wasn't enough food for seconds. I hated having to wear clothes from thrift stores—or worse, hand-me-downs from girls who liked to let you know how rich their daddies were, and how generous they were being by sharing their "old" clothes. Watching my mother face one crisis after another as my father worked hard as a truck driver, and watching them both struggle in their unhappy marriage, I was inspired to create a different life—a life on *my* terms.

My parents separated when I was a teenager, and went on to other relationships. I didn't really fit in with either of these new families, so three weeks after I turned sixteen, I moved out on my own. Stepping out into the "real world," I realized that life is a series of doors we walk through, and that the only people we can count on are ourselves.

My dad had always impressed upon me that education was the key to creating what I wanted. I graduated high school early, and went on to college. They say that when one door closes, another opens— that we can be as happy as we choose to be. I chose to look for the open doors. It wasn't always easy, but I kept my goal in sight: financial security, and eventually a family to share it with.

I was blessed with great teachers, and graduated college early as well. My first job in corporate America was as executive assistant to the CEO of a Fortune 100 company in Los Angeles. Our company was a sponsor of the 1980 Olympics, and one of the highlights of my job was the opportunity to be part of the Olympic planning committee. Although it was exciting, I loved a good challenge, and soon I was looking for another open door.

When I received my degree in finance, I was off and running in my second job as a financial analyst in Beverly Hills. This job started out small, with just a few simple reporting responsibilities, but it grew to include interviewing mutual fund managers, state senators, and even the Governor of California, as well as supervising the entire client reporting department. I wrote a syndicated newspaper column, traded billions of dollars in U.S. Treasury bonds, and analyzed tax-advantaged investments for high net worth individuals and companies. The work was fast-paced and paid well, and my boss challenged me every day. I loved it so much that I literally became married to the job.

In every career, there are unique lessons. As a financial analyst and behind-the-scenes researcher and writer, one of the best lessons I learned is that a woman will more than likely be single at some point during her life. A few will never get married, quite a few will get divorced, and many will outlive their spouses. I witnessed first-hand that most women—in truth, most *people*—don't have a back-up plan, a "Plan B." In fact, 97% of our population ends up broke by age sixty-five.

This made it very clear to me that I needed to have a plan for my life—because when you fail to plan, you plan to fail. No one else was going to take care of me, so I needed to take better care of myself. I wondered, "What if my primary source of income disappeared tomorrow?" If that was truly a possibility, I had better start creating a life I loved—and make a very good plan.

At that point, I wasn't married; I was supporting myself on my own, as I'd always promised myself I would. But although I loved my job and the security it gave me, there was price to be paid for it. While I enjoyed my front-row seats to concerts and sporting events, rode in limos and private jets, and commanded a huge salary, other areas of my life were suffering. I'd recently been diagnosed with fibromyalgia. I realized that if I kept hurtling down my current path, not only would my dreams of a family be forever kept on hold, I would eventually reach the point where I was unable to work at all.

It was time for a new door.

My diagnosis caused me to look at my life differently. I realized that time is a precious commodity. Since I was sixteen, my biggest goal had been to be a wife and mother. I thought it was important to establish myself financially before settling down, but I knew now that I wasn't on track to the "happily ever after" I had envisioned. Driving home after another long day, I realized that if I wanted a family and my health back, I needed to find another line of work.

I was dating a slightly irreverent attorney, who soon became my fiancé. He mentioned that he wanted to move to Ft. Lauderdale to be closer to his family, and I agreed that his plan had possibilities. I was tired of getting up early, sitting in traffic, working like a dog, and making my boss wealthy. My job was no longer my top priority. If I wanted to start a family, I had to find a way to become healthy again. Plus, I was looking forward to the beach!

Traditional doctors wanted to treat my fibromyalgia with pain pills, sleeping pills, and antidepressants. Now *there* was a depressing thought for an active thirty-four-year-old woman who had the world by the tail! I decided this was not the right path for me, and after just ten days on those toxic meds, I found my real road to recovery in nutritional products.

Once my health improved, I started working on my career. Instead of thinking about my ideal job, I thought about what I wanted my life to look like, and how (and with whom) I wanted to spend my days. I even took money out of the equation. After a lot of research, I chose the network marketing industry. Several friends had created incredible lifestyles in this industry, and I wanted to work with the company whose products had made such an incredible difference in my health.

In a little over two years, I have been able to replace a six figure income working in a career that makes a difference in others' lives and keeps me healthy at the same time. Making my own hours gives me the freedom to be the kind of mom I always dreamed of being. I have finally created the life I dreamed of as a little girl. Not only do I contribute to the financial security of my family, I have time to be the room mom, cookie mom, and field trip mom. Our children know firsthand the benefits of being an entrepreneur, and have learned to be encouragers, negotiators, team players, and good marketers. They're flexible and generous, and I'm proud of them. Their skills and vibrancy will empower everyone whose lives they touch.

When I started this journey sixteen years ago, I never in a million years would I have thought that I would get paid to travel the world, meet amazing people, and empower others to live their goals and dreams. What I do isn't just for me—it makes a difference in people's lives. Now that's juicy!

Juicy Questions

Does this story speak to you? The journaling prompts below can help you access messages from your authentic core, and integrate the richness and insights of this story into your own juicy, joyful life!

Are you married to your job? How does this affect the rest of your life—your family, your relationships, your health?

_____

_____

_____

_____

What does your ideal life look like? If you continue doing what you're doing, will you still get where you want to go?

_____

_____

_____

_____

Sometimes, all it takes to find a "new door" is the willingness to see one open before you. Where in your life do you need a new door?

_____

_____

_____

_____

A New Chapter

Bonnie Ross-Parker

I t was just a checkup.

I showed up for my routine annual visit to my doctor, and while I had been experiencing discomfort and my gut instinct told me something might be wrong, when I heard the word "hysterectomy," I was shocked! There was no time to wait, no time to think. No time to consider other possibilities for treatment. My doctor's advice was clear: now, not later.

I replaced panic with prayer and placed my faith in my doctor. I just wanted to get it over with and move forward with my life.

It was April of 1983. I had been teaching for twelve years, and was already worn out from my classroom responsibilities. The kids were becoming less cooperative by the year, and their parents less supportive. Increased administrative demands already had me thinking about making a change. My sudden medical emergency gave me an unexpected window of time to examine my life and plan what I wanted to do next. I applied for and received ninety days of sick leave, and a year's sabbatical. For the next three months, I would still get paid my full salary, and my only responsibility was to provide lesson plans.

There were no complications, and I recovered quickly. At thirty-nine, I hadn't planned for more children, and hormone replacement caused few if any side effects—but there were still major changes taking place in my life. The thought of returning to the classroom became less appealing as time passed. I knew there was something else out there for me which would prove both challenging and rewarding. And so the search to find my new career began.

One day, I spotted a small business opportunity in my local newspaper which piqued my curiosity. It read, "Innovative franchise looking to expand in Washington, DC." I picked up the phone, and a week later a large packet of information arrived.

As I read the material, I could feel the rush I would get from owning a business, building a dream, and creating a different future for myself. With complete faith, I made the financial and emotional investment necessary to purchase a franchise, and also negotiated the right to be the Area Developer for Washington, D.C. Admittedly, I was a little scared, but at the same time I felt empowered and energized. Friends thought I was crazy to give up a steady paycheck, guaranteed employment, and days off for snow—but for me, the excitement and challenge far outweighed the risk. I *knew* I would be successful.

What began as an annual checkup became a catalyst for significant change in my life, and I embraced it as such. But as I would soon discover, running a business is quite different from running a classroom. At first, I was overwhelmed. It was a huge adjustment to go from lesson plans to P&L statements; from ordering copy paper to stocking inventory; from earning a weekly paycheck to paying employees first before taking a dime for myself. Despite all this, I not only survived, I thrived! In twelve years, I had opened twenty-eight franchise locations, of which I owned six. Was it easy? No! Was it worth it? Absolutely! It gave me my confidence back, and sharpened my leadership skills.

My biggest challenges during those years didn't come from my stores, or from business growth. It came from the corporate office. The entire corporate team was made up of testosterone. In spite of all my successes, I received little, if any, support from my male colleagues, and even less respect.

In early 1991, I had someone ready to purchase a franchise in an untapped area. We found an ideal location, and submitted the paperwork to the franchisor. Two weeks later, the applicant and location were approved. Training was scheduled, and the building lease was being reviewed for signature. We were very excited—but then, our plans came to a screeching halt. I was served with papers from one of my franchisees demanding the process be stopped.

Although I didn't have the authority to approve any location, and the location we'd selected was not in the complainant's territory, he convinced Corporate Headquarters that the new franchisee would ruin his business and demanded that they withdraw approval for the new location. I was shocked, furious, and determined to stick to my guns. Corporate didn't back me, but I didn't back down. In the end, we ended up in mediation, and my team lost.

The case swept through the organization like wildfire. Area Developers around the country became fearful, my reputation was tarnished, and my local group of twenty-two store owners sided with the prosecuting licensee who, as president of our local association, was both outspoken and influential. It didn't seem to matter to anyone but me that he'd distorted the facts.

The next several months were painful and embarrassing. I was devastated. I imagined that everyone was talking about me behind my back. After twelve years of working on behalf of the franchisor, sticking my neck out in support of the female Area Developers, and creating a network that ranked in the top twenty-five nationwide, I was stripped bare. My confidence slipped, and I lost interest in the entire operation.

The one bright light in my life during this time was the man I was dating. Phil stood by me through the entire ordeal, weathering my anger, disbelief, and disappointment with equanimity. In 1995, we were married, and Phil accepted a challenging new opportunity in Atlanta. Glad to have the chance to start fresh, I hired a business broker and sold my entire organization.

While Phil and I didn't know what to expect as newlyweds in a strange city, sharing this experience fueled me with new energy and excitement. As my husband went to work as the CEO of a struggling company, I decided that my new role would be as a supporter and mentor to businesswomen trying to achieve their dreams. I networked like crazy. For three years, every Tuesday morning, anyone who showed up at The Atlanta Bread Company between 7:30 and 9:00 a.m. would find me there, ready to help. I loved it! The rewards far exceeded any paycheck. My self-respect returned, my confidence soared, and my enthusiasm was reborn.

243

Subsequently, I became the Associate Publisher of a local newspaper and created a section called *Women to Women: Cultivating Our Community*. Our women readers offered their expertise, and content poured in.

In 2002, I accelerated my plan to support women looking for business opportunities, or those already in business. I founded *The Joy of Connecting®*, a licensed customer acquisition/marketing program. It's a nationwide, non-membership organization for female entrepreneurs, business owners, and professionals eager to learn about products and services, expand relationships, and foster business growth. Finally, I had created my missing piece. I could utilize all of my training skills to ensure that women everywhere had access to the resources they needed to live their dream of financial independence. My heart was singing a happy tune.

So, where am I today? Well, I'm happy to say that this former schoolteacher has blossomed into a multi-dimensional entrepreneur, living life as an advocate and cheerleader for her sisters! I am a working example of what is possible when we focus, take action, and chart our own course. Despite all the painful and discouraging moments I endured during my years in franchising, I look back with gratitude, knowing that the lessons I learned were the tools I needed to move forward. That chapter of my career is over, and the new chapters I'm creating are the best yet.

Juicy Questions

Does this story speak to you? The journaling prompts below can help you access messages from your authentic core, and integrate the richness and insights of this story into your own juicy, joyful life!

Bonnie's medical emergency was the catalyst for her to change her life. What dreams do you put on hold, waiting for another day? What would it take to make you claim them now?

_____

_____

_____

_____

Sometimes, what seem like our greatest failures are in fact the keys to our success. When has a painful, disappointing, or embarrassing moment spurred you to do something different and better?

_____

_____

_____

_____

How can you use the compassion and wisdom gained from your most trying moments to inspire others? How can you help others by sharing your own mistakes?

_____

_____

_____

_____

Love, COMPASSION, AND Feminine POWER

Queen of Joy

Louise Rouse

I n the wee hours of the morning, I am laughing in the hot tub with my girlfriends under a full moon. We are together to celebrate the completion of my dark night of the soul.

My sisters ask, "How did you find happiness again?"

There is a rainbow around the moon from the mist in the sky. My mind drifts to thoughts of my mother, who I think of as the Queen of Joy. I've often heard her speak of the moon as if it were one of her lovers. Her eyes light up like stars in the sky as she tells of her passion for it; she feels that the moon speaks to her, and fills her very being with a connection to the magnificent Universe. Watching the moon and hearing my mother's voice inside me, I know exactly how and why I've been able to embrace joyous living.

I share my reflections with my girlfriends, and tell them about the three most important lessons my mother taught me. First: form a deep connection with, and appreciation for, the wonders of the Universe. Second: cherish your girlfriends and the Feminine. Third: when all else fails, chocolate will make everything better.

One of the ways my mother connected to the universe was through gardening, but when she was extremely upset, she would pack all the kids in the car and head for the beach. As soon as we arrived, she would run to touch her feet to the sea. Breathing deeply of the ocean air, with tears streaming down her cheeks, she would tell us, "The ocean is very healing."

When the ocean was not an option, we ate chocolate.

After my twenty-two-year-old son died suddenly of a heart attack two years ago, I turned my whole kitchen into a chocolate factory. I made one hundred sixty four jars of syrah chocolate syrup. Chocolate was everywhere. It was all over my stove, the floor, and me. I learned that, while making chocolate, you have to watch it every single minute: if you turn your back, it bubbles all over everything faster than you can say "Holy Smokes!" It was in this hysterical, sad, chocolaty moment that I realized I was in deep trouble. There was not enough chocolate in the world to ease my pain.

Desperate to feel connected with the universe again, I remembered the fourteen angels. About a year before my son's death, I had discovered *The Essene Gospel of Peace, Book 2* by Edmond Bordeaux Szekely. The book translates the Essenes ancient knowledge from Hebrew and Aramaic scripts found in the Vatican's basement by a janitor.

I started rereading the book, hoping it would help. From the very first chapter, I thought of my mother. Although she is not religious, she is a woman of simple values, and I knew she would appreciate the Essene wisdom, which teaches basic principles in a profound way. Know that God is love. Honor the Ten Commandments. Commune every morning and every evening through one of the fourteen angels.

Throughout the previous year, I'd faithfully communed with the angels, but I'd lost the thread in the midst of tragedy. Fortunately, I remembered that these angels are my guides, my connection to the Divine. They create a conduit to facilitate miracles; certainly, I thought, they could help me pave a path to my son.

In an act of faith, I created an altar under an old madrone tree. I adorned the branches with wind chimes, and placed a statue of the Mother Mary beneath. I called the madrone tree my "listening tree;" it became a sacred place where I could connect with my son. There, I sought answers by opening my heart with ears to hear. I asked for forgiveness, and opened my eyes to see. Under the moon, I cried and opened my soul to sing. My songs were like a portal that opened the veil to the other side. With every new phase of the moon, I built a new relationship with my son. The morning angels kept me grounded, while the evening angels gave me hope.

I asked, and received. The answers came on the wind blowing sweetly by my side, on the sound of a wind chime ringing, or on the back of a shooting star. In the darkness I listened, and through listening light was revealed. While everyone else was sleeping,

I was awakening. The bridge between the two worlds was swept away. I witnessed the mist of the soul; I felt and saw the quantum energy which never dies, only transforms. I learned to let go of my son's physical being, and began to make room for a new invisible relationship.

Images of hills alive with music ran through me—like I was Julie Andrews in *The Sound of Music*, my mother's favorite movie. My connection to the other side was deeper than hope or dreams; it was empowered with the joy of certainty. I could feel it, and others could see it.

On one girls' night out, my girlfriends told me they could see happiness bubbling out of me. When I arrived home later, the listening tree was waiting for me. In the midst of processing my newly found joy, a wave of guilt washed over my happiness, stopping me in my tracks. "Is it okay to be happy?" I wondered. "Is it okay to let go of grief?"

Once again I poured out my heart and soul to the listening tree, and asked for an answer. I needed an absolute sign, one that was unquestionable. I told the tree, and my son, that if all the wind chimes rang together, I would know it was okay to be happy.

I stepped back and waited. At first, the world was utterly silent. But then, a great gust of wind came rushing by, so strong that the tree branches bowed in the breeze. The chimes sang with music, and I wept in gratitude, thankful for my answer and for my invisible relationship with my son.

Back in the hot tub, my girlfriends ask me to share more about the angels and the ancient wisdom. I tell them about a random survey I once conducted, where I asked one hundred people if they believed in God. Almost all of them said yes. Then I asked, "Under what conditions do you feel God's presence?" Most replied that they felt God when they were in nature. Communing with the angels, I told my sisters, is a lot like communing with God in nature. The angels are described by the Essenes as the Tree of Life, powerful guides for healing our dear Mother Earth. The angel with us tonight is the moon: eternal life. My mother's angel.

251

Giggling in the moonlight, my sisters are like the branches of a tree. Each follows her own path, yet we all are connected. All though the evening we have danced, and talked. We've shared freely, without the need for explanations, and completed each others' thoughts when words were lost. We've opened and closed doors with hot flashes, rubbed each others' necks and feet, and shared bites of dark chocolate. We've savored the richness of life, a richness money cannot buy, and refreshed our spirits in preparation for the days to come. I feel a rush of joy thinking of my mom, who was always so grateful for her own girlfriends. She would smile to see us here tonight.

Before leaving the hot tub, my sisters and I take turns declaring our intentions for the month. After each sister shares her vision, she kisses the back of her right hand and sends her intentions to the angel of the moon. As I kiss my own hand and send my intentions, I whisper, "Thank you for letting me be the daughter of The Queen of Joy."

Juicy Questions

Does this story speak to you? The journaling prompts below can help you access messages from your authentic core, and integrate the richness and insights of this story into your own juicy, joyful life!

We all inherit traits, thought patterns, and coping mechanisms from our parents and parental figures. What positive inherited patterns stand out in your life? How can you honor these gifts?

_____

_____

_____

_____

Do you feel closest to your divine guidance in nature, or in some other setting? How does spending time in closeness to your Divine power enhance your life?

_____

_____

_____

_____

Many of us discover, or rediscover, our spirituality during painful periods in our lives. How have the trials in your own life enhanced your relationship with your higher power?

_____

_____

_____

_____

The Language of Compassion

Sue McPhee

She wafted into the hospital room, graceful, efficient, moving about her duties with a buoyancy that surprised me. She appeared to be in her late thirties, with long dark hair that she wore pulled back from her face. She whisked through the room with her mop and a pail full of nothing but water, and scrubbed as if it were the most important work she would ever do.

This was the ward for abandoned babies in the pediatric building of a Romanian hospital. These babies were not particularly ill, but their mothers had left them there anyway. We were told it was common. They'd bring the babies in for care, inform the nurse they'd "be right back," and then simply disappear. Hearing this, my heart sank. These poverty-stricken mothers knew where their babies could be provided for. With pain in their hearts, they would leave; leave out of love, leave out of necessity.

Down the narrow hallway, I caught another glimpse of the cheery nursing assistant. She seemed so upbeat that it shamed me. Could I be so cheerful in the midst of this intensity? I guessed it was a matter of perspective. Knowing little Romanian, I tried to communicate with her anyway, making a feeble attempt in my very rusty French.

Her eyes lit up: she understood. The bond of communication had been established. I learned that her name was Angela, and she worked there every day.

I wanted so much to continue our chat, but my attention was diverted by our mission. I hoped I would run into her again.

There were three other women in the infant room—my teammates, fellow volunteers from the U.S. We had arrived in Romania, along with eight others, just three days earlier. Our assignment: to bring the gift of infant massage instruction to Romania.

It became so much more.

Following a bumpy van ride through the ghetto streets, we had been welcomed into town by an amazing and energetic woman. Jeni, who ran a parenting center, was to be our hostess and guide. She paved the way for us to teach the caregivers at the pediatric ward, the workers at the orphanages, parents in their homes, and mothers who came into the center. It was a lot to accomplish in fifteen days.

We had daily opportunities to learn about our hostess. We were touched by Jeni's humility as she spoke of her beloved Romania; its past, its present, and its potential future. She spoke of difficult living conditions, typical family meals consisting of nothing more than pig lard and bread, babies abandoned by mothers, and the economic status of the struggling community.

Listening to Jeni talk, my thoughts drifted back to Angela. I wondered what her life was like, and what she had to do to survive. I looked around the room and noticed that many of my new sisters were, as I was, having a hard time holding back the tears.

Then, unexpectedly, Jeni handed us each an invitation. During the course of our work there, she said, we would inevitably meet and get to know several Romanian women. Each of us was to choose one woman to invite to a small reception. There was no doubt in my mind who my invited guest would be: Angela of the dark hair, sparkling eyes and dauntless enthusiasm. Angela, my new-found Romanian French-speaking friend. I could hardly wait to tell her.

The days of our mission progressed, and we continued our wonderfully gratifying but emotionally draining assignments. One morning, we got up early in order to get to the infant ward before 8:00 a.m. We would attend to the babies right after their morning baths, and this would give us a better insight into how the workers might be able to incorporate the infant massage.

When we arrived, the babies looked much brighter and more alert. Also, they were dressed differently, in outfits that allowed for more movement. On a previous visit, we had removed their bindings in order to perform massage, and the effects of our interventions were already evident. We felt joy to see the fruits of our labor realized, but it was, as always, tempered with sadness for the difficult life these babies would inevitably face.

We got right to work, and what a sight we were: a bunch of surrogate mothers, holding, feeding and loving these beautiful waifs. But even as I worked, couldn't help thinking about Angela. Would I run into her that day? Would I get a chance to hand her my invitation?

Suddenly, she entered the room, her smile filling the space with love and cheeriness. She was overwhelmed to receive the carefully printed and folded invitation. Her face radiated a surprise and warmth I will never forget. You would have thought I'd handed her an invitation to the most exclusive dinner party in all of Eastern Europe! Again, I realized how much perspective can change things.

After several more days of joyous yet heart-wrenching work, the day of the reception finally arrived. Angela, of course, had accepted my invitation, and since then we had really hit it off in our communication—which was partly Romanian, partly French, and a little English, but mostly the universal language of compassion. I was looking forward to honoring her that evening; honoring her for her good nature, her hard-driven work ethic, and above all, her compassion for the babies.

The morning of the event, I had purchased a beautiful hand-embroidered outfit in the village, and I chose to wear it for the first time that evening. I truly looked Romanian. When Angela arrived, I was thrilled and amused to see that she'd chosen an above-the-knee outfit of silken material, nylons, and high-heeled shoes, and looked *very* American! What a sight we were! The humor and poignancy of the moment was not lost on us, and we giggled like schoolgirls.

Soon, the other women began to arrive, and the chatter escalated. Jeni began with a greeting; then, a Romanian nurse from the hospital stood up and began a beautiful soliloquy, expressing profound gratitude for the work we had accomplished since our arrival. It was humbling. As if her speech was a cue to the others, one by one our new Romanian friends followed suit. It was an amazing meeting of minds and hearts, women to women. Angela and I held hands in friendship and mutual understanding; two women, worlds apart, who might never see each

257

other again. I realized that I needn't know more of Angela's life; her presence in that room spoke volumes.

As the evening drew to a close, we sat in silence, tears pooling in our eyes. Then, Angela reached for a bag she had been carrying throughout the evening, and handed it to me. She had brought me a gift of crystal from her home, probably a cherished item she'd had for years. I knew it would be an insult to refuse it. A lump formed in my throat. She had given me so much more than that piece of glass. I shook as my hands cradled the delicate symbol of our friendship.

After returning home, I wandered around in a daze. I was functioning—at least, I was getting up and going to work and brushing my teeth—but I felt like an outsider. Before this trip, I'd believed that I was spiritually and emotionally mature enough to understand the true nature of compassion. After all, didn't I help people? Didn't I volunteer my services frequently and selflessly? I thought I had voided myself of materialistic behavior and selfish nuance, but in reality, I had barely scratched the surface. I had been looking at my personal development through narrow lenses, fixating on a very small circle of existence. And then Romania happened: Romania, with its painful past, and its poverty-stricken yet cheerful and generous people.

I was ashamed that it had taken this huge step out of my reality for me to learn that compassion is as simple as a single non-judgmental kindness; that happiness and fulfillment come in tiny packages of faith, hope and love; that a smile, radiating from my deepest core, can heal more surely than any treatment or philosophy I could impose; that each time I am privileged to touch another human life, there exists an opportunity to leave a new speck of illumination.

Today, I know that we don't need something as big as a mission to a foreign country to teach us these lessons. We need only open our eyes and hearts to really see what lies before us, and really listen to what is being said. Opportunities to speak the language of compassion are everywhere.

It's been ten years now, and still a word, a song, or a feeling can instantly catapult me back to the joy, the love, and the sorrowful beauty that is Romania, and my memory of Angela.

Juicy Questions

Does this story speak to you? The journaling prompts below can help you access messages from your authentic core, and integrate the richness and insights of this story into your own juicy, joyful life!

Often, moments of revelation come when we set our own interests aside in order to work toward a greater goal. Have you had such an experience? What did it teach you?

_____

_____

_____

_____

How do you define compassion? How has compassion given or received positively affected your life?

_____

_____

_____

_____

Sue's story demonstrates that we can use the universal language compassion to create a bridge between ourselves and someone whose experience differs from our own. With whom can you communicate in this way?

_____

_____

_____

_____

Women's Wisdom

Judy Ann Foster

“There is a magnet in your heart that will attract true friends. That magnet is unselfishness, thinking of others first... When you learn to live for others, they will live for you.”
— *Paramahansa Yogananda*

I guess you could say that the real "juiciness" in my life comes from meditation. I cannot think of anything else which has meant so much to me as the pursuit of the spiritual and the delving into the mysteries of who we are. For as long as I can remember, I've been a seeker, and very early on I had the inkling that inner peace, centeredness, and intuition were the keys to fulfillment.

As a young woman in the 1970s, I discovered the teachings of Paramahamsa Yogananda—the amazing Indian Yogi who, in the 1920s, brought the wisdom of the East to the West. I attended meetings of Yogananda's Self-Realization Fellowship, and was so enthralled by what I learned about meditation and the principles of an enlightened life that I wanted to join SRF's monastic community. The nuns smiled at me when I expressed my desire to "give up all." Somehow they knew that my path was to be in the world—and there was no conflict with that, because Yogananda's teachings also apply to people who live active lives in the world.

I worked with SRF for many years, and devoted myself to the spiritual practices which, to this day, are the backbone of my life. But the monastics were right—my path was in the world. For starters, there was my deep love of children, which led me to my path as a teacher. I embraced one of the world's most creative and child-centered educational programs—the Montessori method—and by 1991, I owned two Montessori schools. This was satisfying work, and enjoyed my newfound sense of business success.

I'm a soft-spoken person, so I found it bemusing when friends would say, "You know, Judy, you could be the CEO of a company." Being a CEO in the traditional sense, heading up some kind of corporate organization, was not at all what I wanted. But I do feel that my friends' observations about my organizational abilities were the outward reflection of an inner process I had been going through for some time. Much as I loved my work, I yearned for something much different than teaching at Montessori schools.

Often when people initiate change in their lives, it's the result of some kind of "Ah-ha!" moment, or some learning that arises from a crisis. But my yearning for "something more" arose as part of a gradual process—which itself evolved out of my regular practice of meditation. Long before, I'd learned that listening to my intuition, even if I didn't fully understand its prompting, was the best way to find the "more." So when a deep part of me longed to connect with other women—with feminine wisdom—I felt the beginnings of a calling to bring the women in my life together to share our successes and express our gratitude for all the good things in our lives.

At the time, I had no idea how I was going to make this happen. I certainly didn't realize that this idea was to be the seedling which would blossom into an entirely different life mission for me.

One day, I started calling women who I knew might be interested in getting together. A friend agreed to be the presenter. On the following Monday, twenty women showed up for my first event. The energy was incredible: my living room was filled with such love and joy as these women met and connected in the spirit of friendship and sharing. I'll never forget the date—11/11/1991, such a spiritually significant number. This powerful synchronicity let me know I was on the right track.

After that night, I knew without any doubt that my future involved stepping up to a new level of communication. I recall telling my friends that I didn't know why I was following this new path, but I just knew it was the way of the future for me. Of course, I felt some sadness at the prospect of giving up my Montessori schools, but I knew I had to let go and trust the Higher Wisdom.

The Universe agreed! Every week, my gatherings grew. Within two months, there were over forty women crowded into my living room ready to support each other's growth, mastermind about the paths we wished to open in our lives, draw upon our collective intuition, and share our courage and hope. I thought, "This is feminine wisdom at its best!" To me, women's wisdom is juicy and organic. It comes from the heart, and is nourished by the spirit. I found lots of fuel for my own journey into the Divine Feminine by listening to the amazing stories of the women who opened their hearts to one another in my living room. Business owners, authors, mothers, wives, teachers, and healers embodied the wisdom of the eternal feminine for each other. We came together to share our vision of everything life could be, and we wanted that vision to grow!

The name for our group came to me in a sudden flash of insight: as is often the case with long-term meditators, ideas can appear to me seemingly out of the blue. Today the Shared Vision Network—as my intuition led me to call it—has grown into a thriving community of over 50,000 members, both male and female, around the world. When I look back on our beginnings, I am amazed at how naturally it all seemed to evolve. People came out of the woodwork, wanting to be part of a new way of seeing, doing, and being in the world.

263

I didn't set out to create a worldwide organization—I was quite happy with the living room meetings—but the network seemed to gain a life of its own, and I'm thrilled that it has touched so many people. However, because my personal passion has always been focused on feminine wisdom, I created a new name for the groups of women who continue to meet: Women's Wisdom. We currently have over 4,000 members in Southern California, meeting in various cities.

Ever since that auspicious day—11/11/1991—I have been privileged to hear and share so many amazing stories. In Women's Wisdom we learn how to receive Divine Mind, and work together to ask Divine Mind for help. But it doesn't stop there! As I witnessed the fruition of my dream to tap into women's wisdom, my intuition told me that Women's Wisdom should have a global presence. After all, the world needs wise women! Inside us all is a compassionate Presence that can help heal the world of so much of the pain that is happening today. My latest vision came true when, in May 2010 we launched our global initiative, which includes a web site and plans for tele-seminars and other virtual events. Women's Wisdom can now reach beyond the boundaries of geography or time zones.

I look back now and marvel that everything I masterminded in the early 1990s has come to pass. I've learned that when you have a vision that calls you, it doesn't matter if you don't at first see how you are going to make it happen. All it requires is that you walk in trust, one step at a time.

Juicy Questions

Does this story speak to you? The journaling prompts below can help you access messages from your authentic core, and integrate the richness and insights of this story into your own juicy, joyful life!

What do the words "feminine wisdom" mean to you?

_____

_____

_____

_____

Do you have a circle of women upon whom you can rely for support in life and business? How do your wise women make your life juicier?

_____

_____

_____

_____

Is meditation a part of your life right now? Do you think that meditating on your goals allows you to access them more quickly or effectively?

_____

_____

_____

_____

AFTERWORD
Editor's Note

I t's not often that a book comes along with which I can connect on a deep, visceral level. Of course, I see passing similarities in myself to characters, narrators, or themes—but they're superficial, and easily forgotten. Not so with this book.

The authors who have contributed their words, wisdom, smiles, and tears to this anthology have all been my teachers. I found my eyes brimming as I read Kathleen Sims' beautiful story of soul mate love for the first time. I saw my own story played out nearly word for word in Amy O'Brien's "The Safe Path," and I remembered vividly, reading Lynnet McKenzie's "Message in the Mirror," the first time I was able to look in the mirror without cringing.

Tuck Self's light-hearted humor made me giggle, while Sue McPhee's account of compassion in the midst of devastating poverty and sorrow reminded me of the all-encompassing power of love. Shann Vander Leek, with whom I've worked on other projects (including her brilliant new book, *Life on Your Terms*), is an all-around inspiration, and a model for Goddess power. Simran Singh's "Climb Every Mountain" proved to me, once again, why it's important to keep my workaholic predilections on a tight leash.

I wish I had the space to mention every one of our authors here, and share with you the ways in which their contributions have impacted my life over the course of this project. Suffice to say that their stories are amazing, their positivity empowering, and their honesty refreshing. Read them once, and then read them again.

Truth, in its myriad forms, never gets old.

Matsuo Basho said, "Do not seek to follow in the footsteps of the wise; seek what they sought." In the case of the wise women who have shared their stories in *A Juicy, Joyful Life*, we clearly see that many paths can lead to the same destination: fulfillment, joy, passion, peace, and a life created in the image of a dream.

It is my hope that these stories will inspire you not to follow in the footsteps of another, but to seek your own path, following the guidance of a heart made wise by the knowledge that we are all so much more alike than we are different.

Yours in gratitude,

Bryna René
Editor, Inspired Living Publishing, LLC

ABOUT OUR *Authors*

Judy Aleman

Judy Aleman, founder of Soar Beyond Limits, mentors and coaches success-minded women to create greater joy and ease in their lives. Using her Sublime Simplicity process, clients clarify and design a life that fully connects them to their values, passions and vision. A certified professional coach, Judy works with women throughout the nation and offers potential clients a complimentary consultation to explore the coaching partnership. Clients describe Judy as compassionate, insightful, forthright, and committed to their wellbeing and success. For more information, visit www.soarbeyondlimits.com or e-mail judy@soarbeyondlimits.com.

Terri Amos-Britt

Terri Amos-Britt is the author of *The Enlightened Mom* and *Message Sent*, and founder of The Enlightened Mom (www.theenlightenedmom.com), a global healing community where moms unite to heal the world. As a spiritual coach and inspirational speaker, Terri shares her experiences as a wife, mom, stepmom, widow, and former Miss USA and television host, teaching moms tools to shift their lives from pain and suffering to peace, abundance, wholeness and joy. And as mom heals...the family heals...the world heals.

Ellie Bassick-Trovato

Overcoming her lifelong struggle with weight and depression in the wake of her husband's and father's deaths, Ellie Bassick-Trovato, now an inspirational speaker and author, has learned that life is only—and exactly—what we make of it. Find out more about Ellie's wellness center, Uplifting Connections, at www.upliftingconnections.com, and learn more about how she can help you live a happier, healthier life at www.asexyconfidentwoman.com or www.elliebt.com.

Donna Cravotta

Donna Cravotta owns Virtual Management Concepts, LLC, offering authors and solo and small businesses assistance with online marketing, social media management, author support, and PR services. Donna and her son Matthew live in the suburbs north of New York City. Find out more about Donna at www.virtualmanagementconceptsllc.com.

Juanita Crawford Bobbitt

Juanita Crawford Bobbitt is a writer. She is also a licensed real estate broker, and enjoyed a distinguished career as a senior officer with the United Nations and has served as a development management consultant. Juanita is a leader in her community, serving on various professional and community service committees, particularly focused upon the empowerment of women and children worldwide. The author of numerous documents on development management, she is currently writing her first work of fiction aimed at inspiring readers to learn about and appreciate their heritage. You can contact Juanita at juanita.bobbitt@gmail.com.

Cynthia deWet

Cynthia deWet is the owner of Adora Wise and co-owner of the Quantum Healing Institute. After nineteen years in alternative medicine and over fifteen years of extensive study, Cindi will soon receive her Ph.D. in Naturopathy and Metaphysical Sciences. She has also earned numerous certifications in a wide variety of wellness principles. Cindi's passion is working with women and families. She loves to help families get out of the "stress cycle" and thrive! Visit Cindi at www.quantumhealingtyler.com or www.spiritquestweb.com.

Joy Earle

Joy Earle is a women's conference speaker and gifted vocalist. She lives her passion by sharing her stories of life's greatest joys and frustrations, calling them "Joy Stories." After reading her blog or hearing her speak, you'll understand why others say she is "so real!" Joy and her husband Jeff traveled for twenty years sharing life lessons on marriage and family; now, she is living a juicy, joyful life investing in women's groups all over the country. Learn more about Joy at www.joyearle.com.

Judy Ann Foster

Judy Ann Foster is the visionary founder of WomensWisdom.net and Shared Vision Network. Since founding Women's Wisdom in 1991 she has been a passionate advocate for empowering women in business and friendship by hosting and producing monthly networking events throughout California. In 2010, Womens Wisdom expanded their live events to provide a global virtual community to encourage women to come together in support and collaboration. Judy lives in San Diego with her husband Ken Foster, just four doors down from her two beautiful grandchildren, who are her greatest joy. Learn more about Judy and Women's Wisdom at www.womenswisdom.net.

Genevieve Kohn

Genevieve Kohn is a life/wellness coach, energy healer, and the owner of Triad Wellness in Medway, Massachusetts. She is also the creator of Healers' Network (www.healersnetwork.biz) and conducts workshops around New England. Genevieve lives a juicy, joyful life in suburban Boston with her husband and two young sons. She can be reached at (877) 4-TRIWEL [(877) 487-4935)], or by e-mail at info@triadwellness.net. Download the Free Report at www.triadwellness.net!

Sue Landis

Sue Landis created the Live Bold Project to inspire women to experience a deeper level of authenticity by being accountable to their dreams. She also has a breakthrough program to help women achieve their health goals, contributing to an amazing improvement in their vitality and energy. Sue is also a motivational speaker, and successful real estate broker in Carlsbad, California where she lives with her husband Steve and daughter Sophie. Meet Sue at www.liveboldproject.com.

Caia Martin

Caia Martin is a laughter yoga instructor, EFT® practitioner, life coach, mother, and friend. She is the owner of Élan Health and Wellness, a resource center for women designed to inspire living a healthy, well balanced life, and the author of *Dream It. Live It!*—an introspective workbook developed to help anyone uncover their passion and purpose. Find out how you can live your most abundant life at www.elanhealthandwellness.com, or contact Caia at caia@elanhealthandwellness.com.

Roseanne Masone

An avid SCUBA diver, underwater photographer, and snow skier, Rosanne is the founder and CEO of Giant Strides LLC, a company promoting personal empowerment through positive living and life coaching. Author of *Chasing the Shark: A Journey from Fear to Freedom*, she is a former Fortune 500 company corporate director and law firm office manager, and is listed in the Metropolitan Who's Who. She is also a licensed real estate agent and an Herbalife International Wellness Coach. You can find Rosanne on the web at www.giantstridescoaching.com, and contact her at rosanne@giantstridesllc.com or (888) 220-2727.

Laurie McAnaugh

Laurie McAnaugh, M.Ed., CLC, is an experienced teacher, coach and leader, and the founder of Access Your Power. She believes that a strong sense of self is the single most important quality you will ever create. She encourages people to view the situations and relationships in their lives with a new attitude, while using this higher perspective to grow and influence others. Her clients develop tools for empowerment and enjoy higher levels of self-confidence. Find Laurie on the web at www.choosetobepowerful.com.

Lynnet McKenzie

Lynnet McKenzie is known as the Empress of Ecstasy. She is a master at locating and clearing the crud that blocks the ecstasy of the soul. She's an intuitive healer, divine channel, body story expert, ecstasy coach, and single mom. Her passion is to empower others to live their passion. She leads workshops and virtual group coaching and hosts a weekly radio show, Opening to Ecstasy, on the Transformation Network. Contact Lynnet via www.openingtoecstasy.com.

Sue McPhee

Sue McPhee, C/LMT, RMT, has been practicing in the intuitive and healing arts for over twenty-five years. Four of those years were spent in New York City ghettos treating multiply-handicapped and underprivileged infants and children. A highlight of those years included a fifteen-day medical mission to Romania to teach infant massage in the heart-wrenching orphanages and poorly-funded hospitals. Following this journey, she vowed to "never whimper and complain; never snub a simple meal or a humble conversation." You can reach Sue at (603) 464-5119, or visit her web site at www.suemcphee.massagetherapy.com.

Kate Michels

Kate Michels: Core Alignment Specialist, internationally recognized facilitator and instructor, Making Miracles Bonding Before Birth Coach, Neuro Linguistic Practitioner, Parent Coach, Dream Coach Group Leader, Life Blueprint Specialist, Head Coach Trainer for SetWeight4life, motivational speaker, bestselling author, Centerpointes LPIP Answerwoman, wife, mother, grandmother, sister and friend. Through years of practical experience with life and clients ranging from babies to people imprisoned for murder, the importance of stories created the foundation for Making Miracles Coaching. Contact Kate at castlebuildingcoaching@yahoo.com, or call (503) 939-9675. Find Kate on the web at www.corealignmentcoaching.com,

RosaLinda Mueller

RosaLinda Mueller is the Founder of 7Kairos, a real estate investment company involved in the CHOP (Community Home Ownership Program) which allows low-income earners to regain property ownership. Her dream is to convert residences into non-profit homes designed for transitional living, houses of refuge or spiritual retreats. When she's not preparing homecomings for her seven children, RosaLinda manages her husband's law office in Southern California. She is an alumna of the University of California at Berkeley. Find her on Twitter at @7Kairos.

Dianne C. Nassr

Dianne C. Nassr, MSW, LCSW, is the Director of the Dianne C. Nassr Healing Arts Center located in Fall River, Massachusetts. She opened her agency after alternative energy healing techniques helped her heal from a two-year battle with Lyme Disease. She is a trained Thetahealing Instructor, a Reiki Master, and a Practitioner in Yuen Energetics, Matrix Energetics, and Reference Point Therapy. For more information regarding Dianne and Healing Arts techniques, please visit www.nassrhealingartscenter.com.

Amy Beth O'Brien

Amy Beth O'Brien is the author of *Stuck with Mr. Wrong? Ten Steps To Starring In Your Own Life Story* and *Stitches*. She is the founder of the Star In Your Own Life Story with Amy Beth O'Brien web site and blog. She is an author and speaker, and holds an M.S. from the Lesley College School of Management. Amy and her two sons live in Wrentham, Massachusetts. Find Amy at www.amybethobrien.com, on Twitter @amybethobrien, and by e-mail at amy@amybethobrien.com.

Amy O'Connor

Amy O'Connor is a Certified Life and Relationship coach who helps individuals and couples develop confident and fulfilling relationships. Trained through the Relational Life Institute in Couples' Therapy, and with a BA in Psychology, Amy also draws from her own experiences in her sixteen years of marriage to create an approach which is straightforward, refreshing, and empowering. She is the founder of Healthy Heart/Healthy Mind (a brisk walking and talking coaching model for individuals) and Your Healthy Relationship (www.yourhealthyrelationship.com). She works privately with couples and individuals in person or via telephone.

Nancy Olsen

Motivated by her own wake-up call, Nancy Olsen realizes that the ultimate pursuit of happiness doesn't start from a tape or a book, but with the person looking back in the mirror. Nancy inspires you to take inventory of your life, and begin accentuating the aspects that bring joy and happiness. Don't just exist day to day...*Let It Feel Exhilarating!* You can find Nancy on the web at www.exhilaratedliving.com. Contact her at exhilaratedliving@gmail.com, or Twitter @NancyLOlsen.

Margery Phelps

After her mother was killed by proper use of prescription drugs, Margery Phelps made health and wellness education her personal mission. As director of publications for nutriceutical companies, Margery wrote and lectured on nutrition and supplements, created twenty-four cartoon characters to teach children about health through her company Glow Kids, and is currently pursuing a career in health coaching while working on her fourth book, The Mending Map. Find Margery on the web at www.margeryphelps.com, and at www.glowkids.us.

Heidi Reagan

Heidi is a CTA certified personal coach, facilitator, and the CEO of Wake Up Women BE (www.wuwbe.com). Spiritual growth and studies have been her passion and her life purpose is to live with strength and clarity, while being spiritually connected and to help others do the same. Heidi is also the founder and creative mind behind Establish Balance Intention Jewelry, a unique jewelry line that originated out of a desire to remind herself, and her teenage daughter, of their own personal worth. You can reach Heidi at heidi@wuwbe.com.

Lisa Reina-Frommer

Lisa Reina-Frommer has studied Western, Vedic, and Egyptian Astrology. She is a professional Astrologer, Tarot reader, and instructor based in San Diego, California. She conducts readings in person and on the internet at www.stepintothelightreadings. com. She is also a writer: her works can be found at www.youvegottobekiddingme.org.

Rev. Nina Roe

The Rev. Nina Roe is the Founder of AngelsTeach.com. She discovered her life mission in her forties: to mentor and teach inspired souls how to connect with their angels and reclaim the magic of everyday life. For information about online classes, readings and the Living with the Angels™ membership program, visit www.angelsteach.com.

Bonnie Ross-Parker

Bonnie Ross-Parker, a multi-dimensional entrepreneur, is a speaker/author and CEO/Founder of a nationally recognized customer acquisition/marketing program called The Joy of Connecting®. Her books include: *Walk in My Boots—The Joy of Connecting; Y.O.U.—Set A High Standard for Being Human* and *42 Rules for Effective Connections*. Currently, Bonnie combines her energy and 27+ years of networking experience to support female entrepreneurs/professionals and businesswomen. Learn more at: www.thejoyofconnecting.com & www.bonnierossparker.com. Reach Bonnie in Atlanta at (877) 411-6611 or bootgirl@thejoyofconnecting.com.

274

Louise Rouse

Coach Louise Rouse, CPPC, is one of today's leading authorities on the subject of Invisible Relationships. She is recognized for her ground-breaking work in conscious thought busting (www.thoughtbuster.com) and for helping people change their life through changing their thoughts. She is an intuitive visionary coach, speaker, and author, whose views are in high demand. Coach Louise is passionate about guiding others toward a life of joy. For a free audio introducing the fourteen angels, visit www.americasgriefcoach.com.

Dianna Sandora

Dianna Sandora is a fun, fresh, and fabulous freelance writer and blogger, with two blogs that you can find at www.diannasandora.com. As a Toastmaster member, and president for one year, she discovered her passion for public speaking. For more than three years she worked as a motivational teacher and speaker for an adult business class. Her participation in this book will launch her motivational speaking and writing business. To receive your free report, "5 Ways to Reclaim Your Destiny," send an e-mail with your full name to destiny@diannasandora.com.

Tuck Self

Raised to be a perfect li'l southern belle, Tuck Self was "appropriate" at the expense of her own happiness. Her journey has been one of finding and reclaiming her authentic voice. As a sought-after coach, self-proclaimed personal growth enthusiast, and author of *The REBEL-UTION: A Woman's Rebelicious Guide to Freedom, Liberation & Bold Self-Expression*, Tuck inspires her clients to live bold and love it! Meet Tuck at www.therebelbelle.com.

Kathleen Sims

A self-made success through a lifetime of deep and sincere inquiry and rich experiences, Kathleen E. Sims, C.H.T.,C.R.C., has emerged as one of the leaders in the field of love, purpose and creating a "juicy" life. She is a coauthor of the best-selling books *Wake Up Women—BE Happy, Healthy & Wealthy* and *Wake Up—Moments of Inspiration*, as well as a motivational speaker, love and spiritual Life Coach, trainer, and Transpersonal Hypnotherapist. She is committed to helping others live juicy, purposeful lives filled with abiding love. Kathleen can be reached at (925) 674-9003. For a Free SoulMate Consultation, go to www.lifetimeloveconnection.com. You can also check out her other web site: www.the-venus-project.com.

Simran Singh

Simran Singh—a visionary, life coach, 11:11 Talk Radio host, *11:11 Magazine* Publisher, and Founder of BelieveSC and C.H.O.I.C.E. Alliance—establishes creative vehicles promoting personal growth, healing and empowerment. Simran supports individuals in realizing authentic personal expression by tapping inherent power and potential via self-inquiry and conscious choice. You can find Simran at these web sites: Believe...Choices for Conscious Living (www.believesc.com); *11:11 Magazine—Devoted to the Journey of the Soul* (www.1111mag.com); 11:11 Talk Radio (www.1111talkradio.com); C.H.O.I.C.E. Alliance (www.choicealliance.org).

Suzy Spivey

Suzy Spivey wants *you* to live your dreams and create a purpose-full life! As a Certified Coach, Speaker, and TV Host/Producer of Daring to Dream™, Suzy radiates passion, creativity, and contagious enthusiasm. Drawing from the deep well of wisdom actualized through her own journey through life, Suzy facilitates change for those in transition, considering a mid-life redesign, or seeking more meaning in life. Visit www.suzyspivey.com for more information, or contact Suzy at (617) 894-9711 or suzy@suzyspivey.com to get started today!

Tara Sage Steeves

Tara Sage Steeves is a sought-after Dream Realization Coach, the author of *Are You Pregnant with a Dream? Guidebook to Birthing a Dream: Conception to Age 5*, and the innovative founder of The Dream Party®. Tara and her company, Create Your Life!, delight in supporting the creative (and sometimes intimidating) process of identifying, nurturing, and manifesting the life of your dreams. Learn more about Tara and The Dream Party® at www.createyourlifeinc.com.

Kris Steinnes

Kris Steinnes is the Founder of Women of Wisdom Foundation and the Women of Wisdom Conference, created in 1993 in Seattle, WA. To manage this organization, Kris created a circle leadership model, which focuses on shared leadership and rotating responsibilities. She is the author of the best-selling, award-winning book *Women of Wisdom, Empowering the Dreams and Spirit of Women*. Kris is a spiritual leader and teacher of Vibrational Psychology, meditation, healing and manifesting courses. Find Kris on the web at www.womenofwisdom.org.

Amy Thoreson

Amy has a passion for helping others see the greatness in themselves, and wrote her story in order to inspire readers to be their best selves. She is a successful distributor for SendOutCards, and has spoken in front of local groups on listening to the inner voice; her biography and inspirational self-help book will be released in fall 2010. Follow Amy on her blog at ajsunny@wordpress.com.

Shann Vander Leek

Unconventional, spirited, and delightfully curious, Shann Vander Leek is a world-class professional coach and the founder of True Balance Life Coaching. Shann inspires powerful women in transition to accelerate the creation of a life on their own terms, while creating more balance in their lives. She is the author of *Life on Your Terms: The Support You Need to Follow Your Passion from Inspirational Entrepreneurs*. Contact Shann today at (231) 668-9850 or www.truebalancelifecoaching.com to schedule a complimentary Accelerator Session!

Katie Verburg

Kati Verburg is a freelance writer located in Portland, Oregon, often writing about subjects related to self-esteem. Recognizing that her challenges were not necessarily unique to her, she founded Truly B, a media campaign advocating a positive sense of self-worth in women. Kati is dedicated to spreading messages that inspire an awareness of self-talk, personal responsibility, the importance of choice, and all that is beautiful, brilliant, bountiful, benevolent, brave, and boundless about us! Visit Truly B at www.trulyb.com.

Crystal Willms

Crystal Willms, Certified Power Coach® and professional speaker, has been active in the brain injury field since 2002. Her goal is to travel internationally, informing the medical community about the impact of brain injury on the injured person's environment, and to help caregivers and other individuals indirectly affected by brain injury create ways to adjust. With high energy and influence, she continues to provide whole-life coaching to clients with complex cases, including survivors of mild to severe brain injury and their support network. Learn more at www.headwaycoachingintl.com or call (403) 230-1464.

Amethyst Wyldfyre

Amethyst Wyldfyre is known as the Torch of Transformation. She provides Energy Mastery Coaching to evolving entrepreneurs and is a multi-talented and award-winning speaker, author, performer, artist, and alternative healer. Her international clientele includes the leading conscious entrepreneurs of our time. Ms. Wyldfyre has been interviewed on a multitude of radio and TV programs and hosts her own radio show, "Blazing Forth the Light," which features world changers on the leading edge of creating the New Earth. You are invited to receive more information and gifts from Amethyst at www.theenergyjourney.com/gifts.

Debbie Wysocki

Debbie Wysocki is the owner of Women with Dreams, a company that empowers the average woman to create a live she loves by teaching her how to build a profitable business in the network marketing arena. Debbie is a wife, mom, volunteer, wellness educator, real estate investor, author, trainer, and a top producer in the MLM industry. A former Beverly Hills financial analyst who is passionate about helping others succeed, Debbie's motto is "How you do anything is how you do everything!" Meet Debbie at www.womenwithdreams.com, e-mail her at Debbie@womenwithdreams.com, or call (954) 781-6629. You can also find her on Twitter @DebbieWysocki.

Aimée Yawnick

Aimée Yawnick has been mentoring women to make personal growth and development a priority for almost 20 years—first in the Health and Fitness Industry, now as a Personal Coach and Mentor. Aimée helps smart, savvy women entrepreneurs overcome the mindset challenges that prevent them from being successful. By focusing on "first things first," Aimee helps her clients build and strengthen the most powerful tool they have: their relationship with themselves. If you want to make more money and attract more clients, make no mistake: it has to start with *you*! Find Aimée at www.coregrowthanddevelopment.com, or call (781) 956-8584.

ABOUT THE PUBLISHER
Linda Joy

L iving her soul's purpose, Linda Joy is a Conscious Entrepreneur, Publisher, and Inspirational Speaker dedicated to inspiring women to live deeper, more authentic, juicier lives.

In her twenty-year journey from welfare mother to award-winning entrepreneur, Linda learned firsthand the power of passion, courage, and perseverance. She has walked the walk, and believes that there are no failures in life—only lessons to be learned and shared. Her personal journey has inspired other women to believe in themselves and the power of their dreams, and proves that anything is possible when you walk in faith.

Speaking with authenticity, passion, and purpose, Linda has been invited to share her heartfelt wisdom with national audiences, colleges, and women's groups, and through these events provides women with tools and tips to reconnect to their inner wisdom. She has been featured on local and national television shows, and in 2000 appeared on a national NBC talk show taped in Beverly Hills to share her inspirational transformation.

As the Publisher and founder of the premiere inspirational magazine for women, *Aspire.* An avid collaborative networker, Linda has partnered with more than seventy conscious business owners to bring her "Mission to Inspire" campaign to a global audience—and in doing so, has created a conscious business model based on five core values that resonate throughout her life. She recently launched her "Feminine Conscious Business Model for Abundant Success" signature program and products to empower other entrepreneurs to step fully into their passion and purpose with authenticity, ease, and grace while building a successful a global platform.

Linda's dedication to providing a venue for women to share their stories, wisdom, and insight also gave rise to Inspired Living Publishing, and an ongoing series of print and digital inspirational anthologies for women and by women, of which *A Juicy, Joyful Life: Inspiration from Women who have Found the Sweetness in Every Day* is a part. Inspired Living is also a growing publisher for other inspirational authors.

Linda believes that when a woman discovers her true passion, believes in herself, and takes inspired action to move forward, that only success can follow. Her hope for every woman who reads *A Juicy, Joyful Life* is this: that they will, through the heartfelt gifts of these amazing authors and the tools on these pages, realize their true potential, and in turn share their unique wisdom with the world.

To Learn More about Linda Joy, visit www.Linda-Joy.com, or Twitter @LindaJoy
To Get Your Free Subscription to *Aspire*, visit www.SubscribetoAspire.com
To learn about upcoming publishing projects, visit www.InspiredLivingPublishing.com.

ABOUT THE EDITOR
Bryna René

B ryna René is a freelance writer and editor dedicated to helping entrepreneurs, visionaries, and spiritual beings around the world bring their messages to light through online and print media. She is the coauthor of *Clean Your Home Healthy: Green Cleaning Made Easy* (with Candita Clayton, Morgan James Publishing, 2008) and *Health Care Dollars and Sense: How Classical Chinese Medicine Can Save Your Health—and Your Bottom Line* (with Dr. Tadeusz Sztykowski, D.Ac., Universal Tao Publishing, 2010), and has edited numerous other successful non-fiction books. Her short fiction has placed in several national and international competitions, and she contributes regularly to *The Providence Journal* and *AAA Horizons*. *A Juicy, Joyful Life* is her first anthology project.

When she's not lovingly molding the written word, Bryna teaches Vinyasa and Prana Flow® yoga at studios around Rhode Island. A lifelong musician, Bryna brings elements of chant and devotional music to her yoga classes.

Find Bryna on the web at www.wordsbyaphrodite.com and www.brynarene.com. Contact her at bryna@wordsbyaphrodite.com, or 401.339.1944.

INSPIRED LIVING PUBLISHING, LLC

...Inspiring the world, one word at a time

Inspired Living Publishing, LLC is dedicated to publishing inspirational stories, titles, and authors whose messages have the power to transform and enhance the lives of others.

At **Inspired Living Publishing, LLC**, we are passionate about providing traditional and non-traditional publishing opportunities which allow women to share their wisdom, stories, and insights with other women across the globe.

At **Inspired Living Publishing, LLC** we believe in the power of the written word to transform lives.

Share Your *Wisdom* in One of Our
Upcoming Projects!

Sign up for our ILP Newsletter for project announcements:
www.InspiredLivingPublishing.com

PO Box 1149 | Lakeville, MA 02347

Mission to *Inspire* 100,000 Women

Claim your **FREE**

ONE YEAR DIGITAL SUBSCRIPTION to Aspire
and bring us *one woman,*
closer to our goal!

OVER 70 BEAUTIFUL PAGES of inspirational content and interviews
from some of today's *leading visionaries*

CONTENT FOR EVERY PART OF A WOMAN'S LIFE:

Life. Purpose. | Body.Soul. Family.Life. | Business. Balance
Aspired Living
and so much more

EACH CONTENT-RICH ISSUE is delivered to your inbox

six times per year

www.SubscribeToAspire.com